Acclaim for Paul Cummins' Previous Books

Dachau Song: The Twentieth Century Odyssey of Herbert Zipper
"I read the book with growing suspense. It is written with crystal clarity and with knowledge of European dimensions rarely found among Americans."
—Sebastian Feldman
Rheinische Post, Dusseldorf, Germany

For Mortal Stakes: Solutions for Schools and Society
"My father, Ralph Abernathy, and my 'Uncle Martin' Luther King would have applauded Paul Cummins, his books, his life's work, and his profound contributions to humanity, as I have."
—Donzaleigh Abernathy, Actress and Human Rights Activist

"*For Mortal Stakes* is rich with ideas and solutions to many of our most troublesome school problems. Educators and citizens alike will find it inspiring."
—Ted Danson, Actor and Environmental Activist

"Cummins offers new visions of education and proven paths to realize those visions."
—Jonathan Kozol

Keeping Watch: Reflections on American Culture, Education and Politics
"A visionary in education who has brought about a bridge for different ethnic minorities to get quality education . . ."
—Arianna Huffington

". . . daring innovation and commitment to the creative process . . ."
—Robert Scheer

A Postcard from Bali (Poetry)
"What one finds when reading Paul Cummins' poetry is that there is no difference between what he does with his poetry and the rest of his life."
—Ann Colburn

God keep me from ever completing
anything. This whole book is but a draught
– Nay, but the draught of a draught. Oh,
time, strength, cash, and patience.
—Herman Melville, *Moby Dick*

Proceed
with
Passion

Engaging Students in Meaningful Education

Paul F. Cummins

with

Anna Cummins &

Emily Cummins

RED HEN PRESS LOS ANGELES

Proceed with Passion:
Engaging Students in Meaningful Education

Cover art "Coral Reef" by Herb Alpert

Book and cover design by Mark E. Cull

ISBN 1-888996-80-3
Library of Congress Catalog Card Number 2003098275

Manufactured in Canada

The City of Los Angeles Cultural Affairs Department, the Los Angeles County Arts
Commission, the California Arts Council and the National Endowment for the Arts
partially support Red Hen Press.

Published by Red Hen Press

First Edition

SECOND PRINTING

To the memory of my father, Paul S. Cummins (November 10, 1907 – March 25, 1983) and my mother, Ruth Wenter, (April 24, 1911 – February 10, 2003).

To Bill Graham for his generosity, commitment to social justice and his wonderful sense of humor.

To Herb and Lanie, angels on earth who help make dreams come true.

Acknowledgements

I would like to begin by thanking Jackie Stehr, my new wonderful assistant for her intelligence, humor and for helping in a dozen ways. Working on this project with my daughters, Anna and Emily, has also been a delight.

In my previous book on education, *For Mortal Stakes: Solutions for Schools and Society,* I thanked my many friends and mentors in the schooling world, but I want to add a few here in no particular order: David Bryan, my partner in creating New Roads and the supplier of the title of this book; Nat Trives, my colleague, friend and co-creator of over 30 years; Anita Landecker and Bill Siart at ExEd and Philip Lance at Pueblo Nuevo – my pals in the charter school business; Laurie David for her support and example of passion in action; Arianna Huffington for her wisdom and friendship; Carol Biondi, Jo Kaplan, and Leslie Gilbert-Lurie for their remarkable examples of commitment to underserved youth; Andrew Bridge and Deanne Shartin for teaching me about the world of foster children; Shari Foos for her deep belief in community and for her encouragement; Dan Belin, Chuck Boxenbaum, Lloyd Cotsen, Bill and Ann Lucas, Tony and Gay Browne and Richard Crowell — for their friendship and support over the years; Pat McCabe for saving a school and his commitment to young people; Bill Graham for being the right guy at the right place at the right time and for his friendship and faith in me; Herb and Lani for sharing the vision and for their extraordinary trust and generosity which led us to name the Village in their honor; Dan Zerfas for helping to launch the Village; Hank Koning and Julie Eizenberg for giving shape and aesthetic vision to dreams; David Newman for his devotion to New Roads and the vision of a village; Adam Polk for his research and love of the Village project; Alva Libuser for her intelligent partnership over the years, her thoughtful reading of several drafts and for her own exceptional insights into education and community; Nadia Lawrence for her wise, meticulous and ruthless editing; Adrienne McCandless, for her extraordinary loyalty, hard work, and wonderful sense of humor; Hiroko, Minako, and Maki for their part in helping to dream the Village, and especially Joel Landau, without whose skills, knowledge, passion and care the Village could not happen. I would also like to thank Howard Zinn, Jared Diamond, and Jeremy Jackson for their generous endorsements, as well as the extraordinary New Visions Foundation Board of Trustees for their ongoing advocacy for those who have no other advocates.

Special gratitude to my friends and associates in the foundation and philanthropic world for their support and guidance: Fred Ali; Isisara Bey; Ken Boxley; Helen Burg; Jim Canales; Kip Cohen; Dennis Collins; Bob Daly; Nancy Daly Riordan; Laura Donnelley and John Morton; Peggy Funkhouser; Lou and Kelly Gonda; Larry and Maj Hagman; Margaret Hyde; Irv and Patti Jaeger; Michele Kydd; Chris Lawford; Laurie Levit; Karl and Mona Malden; Theresa Luo; Alan, Peter and Sarah Mandell; David and Rita Milch; Janice Minton; Peter Morton; Peter Norton; Janice Pober; Marcie Polier; Eliott Ponchik; Brian Potiker; Ray Reisler; Lori Rousso, Joel Schumacher; Pauline Stotsenberg; Wendy Wachtel; Lee Walcott; Charles Weingarten; Patrick, John, and Larry Lannan; Frank Lawlor; Bill Johnston; Carolyn Forché; Sharon Korybut; Jaune Evans, and all my pals at Lannan Foundation — all of whom have helped expand my vision of what is "possible." And finally Michele Hickey and Roger Weaver for our ongoing dreaming together.

Paul, Anna, and Emily would like to thank Kate Gale and Mark Cull for their extraordinary helpfulness in bringing this book to fruition. Red Hen Press is a special publishing company with wonderful values.

Finally, writing a book requires family support, particularly from one's spouse. Mary Ann's support comes in many ways, not the least of which is her example of passionate and meaningful service to others.

Emily would like to express her gratitude to her dear friend and mentor, Leslie King, who continues to inspire and support her both in social work, and in life. Additionally, she would like to thank her colleagues Maria Van DeVenter, Claudia Villegas-Avalos and Jason Holmes for their support, friendship and guidance. Finally, she would like to honor teachers everywhere for the many challenges they face and the courage and dedication they demonstrate to children everyday.

Anna would like to thank the following visionaries for their lifelong inspiration and guidance: Andy Lipkis of Tree People for saving an overwhelmed 23 year old from eco-despair; Jody Maxmin from

Stanford University for bringing education to life for countless grateful students; Professors Laura Strohm, Jeffrey Langholz and Lorraine Lomax of the Monterey Institute for International Studies for their dedication to environmental education; Captain Charles Moore of the Algalita Marine Resource Foundation for his tireless crusade against marine pollution; Randy Olson and Jeremy Jackson of the Shifting Baselines Campaign for working to save our oceans while maintaining a sense of humor; and everyone under the sun who dares to dream of a better world.

We suffer from an incurable malady: Hope.
—Marmoud Darwish

Contents

Foreword

Taking even a cursory glance at America's education system will send a shiver down any parent's spine.

The horror stories are so plentiful, "Tales from the Crypt" could do a decade's worth of blood-curdling "after-school specials" and still not run out of material.

We've got Third World level test scores, a massive exodus of qualified teachers, and beleaguered students trying to learn in schools that are overcrowded, decaying, and don't have enough textbooks to go around.

And what is Washington's answer?

Testing, testing, testing. And photo op legislation like the president's prized Leave No Child Behind Act, which is actually more like the Leave Millions of Children Behind, But Hopefully Not Yours Act.

It's enough to leave you in despair.

And then you come across Paul Cummins — a national treasure whom I was blessed to meet seven years ago when my two young daughters began attending one of the remarkable schools he has created.

Cummins is a truly gifted educator — and a force of nature. Passionate, insightful, fearless, and unrelenting in his pursuit of excellence.

As a rule, there are two types of educators: on one side are the dreamers who write books, envision reforms, and design enlightened curricula; on the other side are the nuts-and-bolts implementers who get things done.

Rarely are these distinct characteristics found in the same person. But for over forty years, Paul Cummins has been combining the visionary and the practical, the theoretical and the hands-on.

He has created two private schools, joint ventured in creating four charter school campuses, and is exploring numerous new projects including building an integrated, interactive, inclusive educational village in Los Angeles. And each new project is fired by Cummins' innovative ideas, coupled with his willingness to roll up his sleeves and become involved in the tough day-to-day challenges.

Luckily for us, Cummins writes the same way he teaches: with enthusiasm, skill, and insight.

Proceed With Passion: Engaging Students in Meaningful Education is filled with bold approaches to giving students the ingredients they most lack in their schooling — a sense of purpose, a reason for wanting to learn and, ultimately, a passion to help others.

As any of the thousands of students, teachers, and parents who have been involved with him know, Cummins is a very straight shooter — in life and on the page. As such, this book does not avoid unpleasant realities and squarely acknowledges the political dimension in education and the potential social and environmental disasters awaiting the current generation of students.

In addition, the book provides a delightful bonus: three sparkling chapters written by Paul's daughters, Emily and Anna Cummins.

Together with their Dad, they help point the way to recapturing a sense of meaning in our schools.

— Arianna Huffington

Emily: Do any human beings ever realize life
while they live it? — Every, every minute?

Stage Manager: No (pause) the saints and poets,
                        maybe—they do some.

— Wilder, *Our Town*

I

THE SEARCH FOR MEANING

CHAPTER ONE

Dropping Out/Buying In

Why this farce, day after day?
— Samuel Beckett
Endgame

The desire for meaning still slumbers,
though submerged beneath the
extroversion of American Life.
— William Barrett
Irrational Man

There are many ways to evaluate a public school system that is failing its students, parents, and, ultimately, the whole community. Standardized test scores are the most widely touted, but *not* the best measurement in my opinion (see Chapter 9). One incontrovertible measurement does offer a significant evaluation: drop-out rates. Quite simply, those students who do not attend school cannot be taught. As Bob Chase, the President of The National Education Association writes: "We look across town to wonderful suburban public schools with modern facilities and teaching staffs that are 100 percent certified, many with M.A.s and Ph.D.s. Students achieve at high levels, and 90 percent or more go on to college. But, in about half the high schools in America's 35 largest cities, the non-graduation rate has risen to 50 percent or higher" (*Education Week*, March 13, 2002).

Non-graduation is, of course, a polite term for drop-out. Mr. Chase could have contrasted the urban public school rates with those of private schools in wealthy, suburban areas where the graduation rate is 100 percent with 100% going on to college! He might have noted these other related statistics as reported in 2002:

- ◆ Students in large cities are twice as likely to leave school before graduating than non-urban youth.

- ◆ More than one in four Hispanic youngsters drop out; nearly half of them leave by the eighth grade.

- Hispanics are twice as likely as African Americans to drop out. White and Asian students are least likely to drop out.

- More than half the students who drop out leave by the tenth grade, 20% quit by the eighth grade, and 3% drop out by the fourth grade. <http://www.focusas.com/dropouts.html>

And what do these drop-outs drop into? Focus Adolescent Services provides us with some answers: "The gap between drop-outs and more educated people is widening as opportunities increase for high skilled workers and all but disappear for the less skilled" (Chase, 2). Some further bits of information from their report:

- Recent drop-outs will earn $200,000 less than high school graduates, and over $800,000 less than college graduates, lifelong;

- Drop-outs make up nearly half the heads of households on welfare;

- Drop-outs make up nearly half the prison population.

Why then are the drop-out rates so high in lower income areas? I recently asked this question of a group of juniors and seniors in Los Angeles public and private schools. The students thought they understood why, and offered these explanations:

1. "They are interested in other things."

My translation: They are *not* interested in being required to sit four to six hours a day in crowded classrooms (often 35–45 to a class) with teachers conducting classes they are often not credentialed to teach while trying to maintain discipline. They are *not* interested in listening to lectures or drills about subject matter without apparent relevance to their lives. They are interested in relationships, entertainment media, gang wars, drugs and sex and occasionally sports, but these things mainly happen outside the classroom. So, they drop out to pursue what they *are* interested in.

2. "They are rebelling against their parents." Translation: They want control of their lives, and both school and families represent *being* controlled. Dropping out on the other hand is an action that the students can initiate.

3. "They see no point in it all." Translation: They have no frame of reference suggesting that college can change their lives. No one in their family went to college. They have no conception of what college can provide. Their schools do not have college counselors. They have never visited a college. Consequently, school seems a dead-end; why not end it sooner rather than later?

4. "School just makes them feel bad." Translation: Receiving low grades, being harassed, teased, and bullied by other students, being ignored and sometimes humiliated by teachers, makes school a place associated with negative feelings. School simply lowers many students' sense of self-esteem day after day until — when the depression becomes intolerable — they drop out.

5. "School is not safe." Translation: When they go to school, they may get hurt physically, and are likely to get hurt emotionally. So why go?

These are a few reasons why many inner-city and low-income district students drop out of school. They all have one thing in common, the reason underlying the central argument of this book: Students across the land who do not learn, do not care about school, and drop out "are not engaged in the process." Schooling to them seems meaningless.

How do we address this issue of drop-outs? In attempting to answer that question, I will begin with insights from students I have taught over the years who *do* find their education meaningful. The following are highlights of their responses.

These students acknowledged that the value of education is simply part of the air they breathe. Most of their parents are college graduates who may talk about their college days with fond nostalgia, and who take the children back to their colleges to football games, reunions, and ceremonies. College to them is a place that is imbued with positive values, a place where good things happen. It is also understood that a college education will help you live the good life, as in having a home and a job, a safe neighborhood to live in, travel and leisure, and material comforts. In some families, that good life is defined as a life of reading, attending concerts and plays, and participating in civic affairs. These private school juniors and seniors realized that they are the beneficiaries of a privileged environment, and that, in addition to their family support systems, their school also helps engage them in the educational process. When we spoke, they were clear and emphatic about how this happens.

First and foremost, they cited a faculty of caring teachers who are passionate about their subject matter. The reason why many of their instructors have chosen to teach in private schools is because they wish to teach their own subjects. They know that in overcrowded classes of 35 or more, teachers become mostly disciplinarians and attendance monitors. The close analysis of a Dylan Thomas poem or an in-depth discussion of the causes of World War I give way to paperwork, keeping order, and teaching strictly to the curriculum. Teachers who "think outside the box" will choose to teach where they have 15–20 students in a class; where truancy is simply not allowed; where parent involvement is swift when needed; and where the campus atmosphere is conducive to learning. (Could these conditions ever be universal? I believe so, but that is another matter.)

Students say that what engages them most are responsible and responsive teachers who know and love their subject matter. As one junior girl once told me, "When the teacher cares deeply about a topic, it's hard not to care yourself; it's kind of contagious!"

Equally important as the teacher's passion for a subject is the teacher's knowledge of the subject. Passion without intelligence is of limited value. It is increasingly common to find teachers instructing on subjects they were not trained to teach. Students will become caught up in a subject when they are led down an inviting path that is absorbing, detailed and complex. Often the magic, not the devil, is in the detail, and it is the teacher's own infatuation with the intricacies of a given poem, theorem, or specimen that will capture the student's attention.

Beyond ardor and knowledge is another ingredient critical for involving students in the educational process: the teacher's interest in the students. Most young people are starved for recognition and attention. The ages from five to eighteen constitute a long struggle to define oneself and to gain a positive sense of self. A harsh, critical teacher can be devastating; one who simply ignores or pays scant attention to a given student can be almost equally detrimental. But a teacher who acknowledges the student's self-hood and encourages (en + courage) can make the whole enterprise worthwhile. One caring instructor often makes the difference between a student's dropping out or buying in.

I had the great fortune in my first year of college to have two such teachers. One was a classmate who essentially adopted me. While standing in line to register for the fall semester of 1955, he introduced himself and asked me what I was reading. I looked at him nonplussed and said, "What do you mean? Classes haven't begun yet." He shook his head in disbelief that Stanford admitted such dolts who thought one only read when assigned. I was, in fact, an intellectual dolt accepted to Stanford because of my race, class, and privileged private school background. Jon took me under his wing and gave me books to read and discuss before classes even began — starting with George Orwell's *Animal Farm* and J.D. Salinger's *Catcher in the Rye*. Jon died a few years later in a tragic motorcycle accident, but his influence is with me every day of my life.

My second mentor taught my Freshman Western Civilization class. Daniel Smith, a teaching assistant whose iconoclasm and peculiar behavior doomed him to a short stay at Stanford, played a pivotal role. He cared about my intellectual growth and directly challenged and inspired me to learn. We may all have had such teachers; it takes only one or two to change a student's life. The key element is the caring, the passion, and the attention. In over-crowded, dysfunctional schools it is difficult for teachers to give individual attention, particularly if they carry a teaching load of five classes a day with 35–45 students per class. In my first year of teaching, I had four classes a day of 12–13 kids per class. Between 1961–1968, my first eight years of teaching (in a private school), I had a maximum load of 48 students. I could assign, correct, and return an essay per week! The students wrote over thirty essays a year and read over 10 novels. More important, I had a relationship with almost every one and still see many of them over 30 years later. How could they not become engaged in my subject? I was on fire about the material; I knew my subject matter; I knew each student's name, individual quirks, and needs, and tried to guide each of their efforts to learn and progress. These classroom conditions need to be restored to our schools. If the entire school establishes an atmosphere emphasizing care and concern for each child within, active learning and excited involvement is almost guaranteed. How this is possible is the focus of succeeding chapters.

The juniors and seniors I interviewed recently added yet another piece to the puzzle. It is truly wonderful when teachers are passionate, knowledgeable, and caring, but if they are also aware of and trained to accommodate the different learning styles of individual students, then the process is even more certain to succeed. The work done in the fields of multiple intelligences, independent studies and portfolio assessment is by now fairly well established. Yet, school administrators and staff are notoriously slow to change. *The way it's always been done* exercises a formidable tyranny from which it is difficult to escape. We learn and teach in radically different ways, and the teacher who discovers how to approach each student is far more likely to draw that student into the process. Some students work best in groups; others need extra time to complete tasks (after all, it is not a race); some respond to lectures, others to the written word; some respond best to multi-sensory presentations. Educational systems that implement this comprehensive approach are both rare and effective.

In addition to adapting teaching styles to correspond with each student's learning strengths, we need to provide students with a rich, diverse curriculum to accommodate their interests, talents, and inclinations. When a disengaged student's curiosity is piqued, he/she will often come alive and that new inspiration will spill over into other activities. Consequently, it is essential that schools offer a program rich in academics, arts, electives, physical activities, projects, community service opportunities, and clubs. Ideally, each student will unearth an exciting area.

For each of these positive ingredients of total immersion in school, there is a negative issue indicating what bores, depresses, and repels students. It is not rocket science to know the difference. We must gain a national commitment to provide the funds for these requirements:

- ◆ Well trained, knowledgeable, passionate teachers;

- Desirable, reasonable teaching conditions;

- Encouraging, warm, caring school environments;

- Rich, diverse curricula.

While each item has a price tag attached to it, we have the means to raise the funds. To date, the problem is that we have not raised the awareness to put these into action.

> *The Situation is ironical. More and more concern about communication and less and less to communicate.*
> — R. D. Laing

REFERENCES:

Chase, Bob. March 13, 2002. Editorial in *Education Week*.

Cummins, Paul and Anna Cummins. 1998. *For Moral Stakes: Solutions for Schools and Society*. Bramble Books and Peter Lang Publishing Company.

Focus Adolescent Services <http://wwfocusas.com/dropout.html>.

"Really, I'm fine. It was just a fleeting sense of purpose—I'm sure it will pass."

CHAPTER TWO

Engaging Students: A Seven-point Plan

Hamm: We're not beginning to . . . to . . . mean something?
Clov: Mean something! You and I, mean something?
(brief laugh) Ah, that's a good one!
— Samuel Beckett

We do not know where we are going
But we are on our way.
— Stephen Vincent Benet

Every human being seeks meaning in life. We hunger for a sense of significance, importance, some higher purpose to our lives. Students also crave a higher purpose in their education. What they do eight hours a day, five days a week and between 160–200 days a year needs to make sense in the long run. Telling students at each stage that "you need to do well to be admitted to the next stage, in order to eventually get a job, to buy a home, etc." is not enough to satisfy their hunger for meaning. Purely pragmatic arguments deprive students of the more significant reasons for ordering and enhancing their lives.

Life is short and school is part of life. As a talk show pop psychologist once said, "Life is not a dress rehearsal." Similarly, each stage of schooling should not be mere preparation for the next stage. Each level should be an end in itself; a meaningful experience for every child. School must touch the students where they, at each stage of development, feel life most intensely. If we want students to buy into the process, then at least some portion of their day, and week, needs to deal with issues that concern them.

The statement that meaning ought to be the goal of educational experience brings up several problems for educators. The quest for meaning is complicated by:

1. The inherent limitations of language — compounded by

2. the inevitable subjectivity of each individual, which means that fully accurate communication is never possible — compounded by

3. the apparent relativity of statements of value that appear to be relative to time, place, speaker, and the power of the speaker.

Nevertheless, I am choosing in this book, either cowardly or wisely, to bypass these problems and simply assume that most readers will agree that certain values are essential to human survival. These standards are themselves the yardsticks by which we measure all other values and actions. Among these are justice, fairness, preservation of biodiversity, and survival of the planet and all life forms. Within this book, these value-assumptions trump linguistic, psychological and relative statements about meaning. It is these values which I believe give meaning to our educational ventures.

The question which immediately looms is, "how?" How do we structure and design our schools to communicate these values and to meet the fundamental human need for meaning? Clearly, students need to be *engaged* in the process. This goal is impossible to achieve if they are bored, apathetic, hostile, tuned-out or otherwise *dis*-engaged. Educators have an almost Herculean task, for the mainstream of American classrooms, primary and secondary (and college, I believe) have lost vision and a sense of direction. The proof is in the disintegration of school systems in both the suburbs and inner cities. There is a general and widespread feeling that we have no national purpose other than our expanding consumerism and materialism. Students, even when caught up in the shopping mall mania, must recognize that something is missing. Preparing for tests, amassing GPAs and SATs and APs is not living life at its fullest.

In addition to the problem of educating students in a drifting and fragmented society, especially in demoralized schools in decaying inner city neighborhoods, there is the problem of balancing traditional and progressive styles of education. The older forms of education are imposed from above and from outside the process. The newer forms educational philospher John Dewey suggested come from "an intimate and necessary relation between the process of actual experience and education" (Dewey, 20). What Dewey forcefully articulated is that if we do not consider the powers and purposes of those taught and if we ignore their age-appropriate experiential capacities, then we will lose too many of them. When this disconnect occurs, learning is accidental: "Those to whom the provided conditions were suitable managed to learn. Others got on as best they could" (Dewey, 45). Little has changed since Dewey penned these words in 1938. Some students learn in conventional classroom setting with conventional drills, tests, homework assignments, but many, and seemingly increasing numbers, do not. They realize they are not learning or are not learning material that connects to their personal experience.

Meaningful education occurs when students perceive its relationship to their future. If students fail to perceive the connection between education and their own needs, they become passive or disruptive and fail to learn. True learning requires two crucial and related ingredients: engagement and activity. Without these two ingredients, students at best simply go through the motions, occasionally memorizing enough data to appear to have learned something. More often, however, they become unmoving and unmoved spectators at their own educational bankruptcy proceedings. Detached in the classroom, they may drop out emotionally and then, in ever growing numbers, they leave school, often dropping *in* to more destructive activities involving sex, drugs, gangs, crime, etc. Notice, however, the word "activities." It is part of the human agenda that people need activity. If schools cannot design and encourage involvement and activity, then students will seek it elsewhere.

Engagement is, of course, a two-way street. Usually students will not become occupied unless the teachers are thoroughly absorbed and knowledgeable about the subject matter and some kind of personal relationship has been established. Students will not care to know what the teacher knows unless the teaching comes alive, but it must be in the context of relationship as well. Thus, while the teacher brings the material to life, simultaneously something awakens within the student. The teacher in this sense is what Rollo May referred to as a midwife: "Completely real in being there, but being there with the specific purpose of helping the other person to bring to birth something from within him/her self" (84). Somehow, the teacher needs to guide the student to take his life, classroom or school opportunities seriously. Time being the essential gift of our lives (what Bergson called "the stuff of reality"), the mindset with which we spend our time defines our life. Breaking down the walls of convention, boredom, apathy, and routinization, and then motivating students to become active in their own education is the task, the profound challenge for teachers and schools. As Frieda Fromm-Reichmann used to say, "The patient needs an experience, not an explanation." In education, the students need experiences that activate them. Too often, what we really find are teachers in motion at the blackboard, moving around a classroom full of sedentary students.

It is necessary to return to the concept of time again before moving forward to the role of actual content in achieving involvement, engagement, and activity. A student's "take" on his life or her education is bound up with attitudes toward time. Is a student disconnected from the present moment because of distractions by past crises or defeats? Is the student daydreaming about future success or fantasizing escapist schemes? Is the student looking forward to the future or leaning on the past? These are critical questions and cannot be addressed if the teacher has no relationship with the student. The teacher needn't play the role of therapist, but must be aware of a given student's orientation toward time and thus able to craft assignments and assessments to meet her subjective needs. For example, a student who is experiencing confusion and drifting because of a crumbling family unit due to death, divorce or illness may need the teacher's help to locate himself in time and place. Simple lessons in chronology, perhaps making a family tree, perhaps a local history unit, may help order the student's world. Students feeling lost in their own subjective universe may be helped by defining their personal time and place in the world, by having their personal time "inserted into the social, historical, and cosmic time." When the subjective world becomes confusing, it may help to give that student a greater hold on objective reality. This can only happen however when the teacher and student are in relationship.

When the teacher is attuned not only to individual personality differences in students, but to individual learning modalities, then the I-thou relationship, as described by theologian Martin Buber, is possible.

In such a process, student and teacher are engaged in a reciprocal encounter that transcends sheer utility (grades, homework completed, etc.) and in which the student begins to see the meaning of a given topic in two contexts: the potential importance of the learning in his own life and in his participation in the world at large. Both are necessary to a healthy sense of purpose in life. This sense of purpose often comes from the student-teacher relationship.

In relationship, the teacher is able to guide the student towards experiencing his or her life as real and valuable. Once this occurs, education makes more sense. The student views each assignment and exercise as a means to more fulfilling participation in school and outside life. The living example of the teacher's excitement for this or that subject becomes a yardstick by which the student measures life. The teacher's energy represents a vital ingredient the student wishes to discover within herself. Once the student has made such a commitment to self and to subject matter, everything changes. It begins, often, with relationship: the model, the encourager, the caretaker of education has called the student out. When this happens, knowledge and life takes on new meaning.

So, how then do we achieve this? Later chapters will suggest specifically *where* we believe we can find a sense of purpose, but since this is really the topic of the whole book, this chapter will focus primarily on how, i.e., what processes will give students a sense of involvement and relevance in the process of their own education. We suggest a seven point plan to achieve this transformation:

1. in books and classes;

2. in action;

3. in responsibility;

4. in cooperative, communal projects;

5. in multi-sensory projects;

6. in creative self-expression; and

7. in play.

Books

Yes, it is still possible to provoke student curiosity through books, but, the books themselves must capture students' interests quickly and with some impact. Once a student falls in love with learning, the books can be selected with less of an eye to the quick hook. Initially, students deadened by a trivialized materialistic culture and anesthetized by the profusion of mindless media offerings will need to have their books carefully selected. Excellent examples are J.D. Salinger's *Catcher In The Rye* or Joseph Weisberg's recent (2003) novel *10th Grade* before reading Henry James's *The Golden Bowl*. Before we assign biographies such as *The Education of Henry Adams* or *The Autobiography of Ben Franklin*, we should provide students with contemporary, accessible, and enthralling biographical pieces such as Julia Hill Butterfly's *Luna* (see my chapter on "The Political Dimension in Education"), or Mark Saltzman's *Iron and Silk* — a lively and engrossing account of his martial arts studies in China, or Carl Upchurch's astonishing account of growing up in a ghetto and escaping its influences, *Convicted in the Womb*, or Jimmy Santiago Baca's *A Place To Stand* accounts of escaping the barrio and prison mentalities through the discovery of reading.

Furthermore, our public schools need to spend enough funds to actually provide students with paperback novels and exciting works of non-fiction to take home. How can students develop a love of books if they can never possess any of their own? To cultivate a love of books requires being able to hold a book, turn its pages, make notes in the margins, visit libraries, construct books of one's own, and have readings and workshops at school by exciting authors. All this can be done, but it requires enthusiastic teachers, committed administrators, adequate budgets and funding, and parental support. All are possible, but currently in scant supply. As we will see in Chapter Nine (Testing: Great Is Our Sin), our obsession with testing has clouded our vision and distracted us from *engaging* students in activities which might actually raise their test scores. You can test a non-reader from now until doomsday, but the verbal test scores will remain low if the student hasn't become engaged in reading and understanding. If, however, we show students that their reading connects in some way to their futures, then they will be drawn in. In

Chapter Four, we suggest ways of encouraging students to read about the social issues of their own neighborhoods and cities.

Action

We awaken students to education and to life through action. Engagement requires activation. They must be involved in hands-on, experiential projects and activities. Furthermore, these activities must hold value for the students. Community service is a highly effective way to involve students. At Crossroads School (Santa Monica) and New Roads School (West Los Angeles) in California, we require community service/community action as part of the curriculum. Students select ventures such as volunteering at senior homes, Head-Start centers, or soup kitchens. Their placements are monitored by full-time specialized teachers. If community action is to work, it must be a school commitment just like math or science or English. We also schedule a weekly seminar for guest speakers and community leaders to discuss related issues with the students. As Crossroads is now over thirty years old, we have held ten- and twenty-year reunions, and overwhelmingly are told by graduates that their community service activities represented perhaps the single most critical and absorbing feature of their education.

Students can also combine literature with action to enliven the whole educational enterprise. Reading about poverty in America becomes meaningful when combined with a community service placement at a soup kitchen for homeless people. The word *home-less* suddenly gains its full shocking impact.

Responsibility

Magic occurs in action-oriented programs. Students who may be labeled as irresponsible become more responsible when given appropriate opportunities. Often, the chance to help others uncovers inner resources they never dreamed they possessed. There is an old Sufi story of a man coming to the master. "Master," he says, "I am depressed; what should I do?" The master replies, "Help someone else." Substitute: "Master, I am bored, alienated, uninterested in school, and irresponsible; what should I do?" We infantilize our teens and wonder why they act like infants.

In addition to community service, social and political action, we can inspire responsibility through a host of other activities: peer counseling and tutoring; student designed, funded, written and produced plays, literary magazines, newspapers and yearbooks; student government; and student organized marches, demonstrations, political consciousness-raising forums. These and a host of other projects activate and animate students. Once youngsters come alive in one area of school, it becomes considerably easier to stimulate them in other areas. The key is continuous involvement in undertakings of importance to them.

A year ago, a group of students at New Roads School visited the Los Angeles Zoo. Several students noticed that the elephants appeared to be thin and unhealthy looking. They asked a few questions of the staff, but felt condescended to or ignored. After doing their own-further research they learned that elephants in the wild need twenty miles a day of exercise. The Los Angeles Zoo elephants were getting *one* mile! Their muscles were atrophying. The students wrote a letter to the LA Zoo Commission expressing their strong feeling that those elephants should not be in the zoo, but taken to sanctuaries. They then made a video of the elephants at the zoo, showing one elephant standing in one place for hours at a time swaying back and forth, which elephants in the wild never do. They held meetings at City Hall with their council member, held press conferences and received television coverage. They received, mysteriously, a packet, with no return address, containing vet reports and inter-office memos documenting severe abuse to one of the elephants in the zoo. This led to another press conference at which the District Attorney promised to open an investigation. He did not fulfill his promise. The students are at this writing pressing the new District Attorney to do so.

These students have learned a great deal about how public agencies operate, how difficult it is to effect change, and the important roles perseverance, patience, and determination play in seeking change. These lessons were and continue to be profound. Seeking better treatment of magnificent and abused animals was a fulfilling task. The students came alive and many have remained involved in animal rights and other political and social issues.

At Crossroads School, teenagers expressed curiosity about why the United States is one of only two nations that refuse to ratify the United

Nations resolution on the rights of children. The students initially were outraged. Their anger led to research, reading reports, Internet investigations, writing essays, and creating inter-school petitions. The topic *engaged* them! Many went on to explore other children's issues: child labor; domestic child abuse; child slavery and prostitution; child disease, malnutrition and starvation. Each of these topics led to additional reading, writing, and participation by students who assume that what we ask them to do has some connection to improving the world.

Cooperative, Communal Projects

The animal rights experience and children's rights project captivated our students for a variety of reasons: they believed they were participating in a significant issue; they assumed and carried out responsibilities; and their actions were cooperative and communal. Few people work at jobs that don't interact with other individuals. Yet, too often schools impose individual assignments and projects of a solitary nature: writing term papers; taking standardized tests, preparing solo oral reports, etc. In most post-school experiences — at work, in sports, in religious or performing groups — people are required to work in concert with each other. Furthermore, advantages both to learning and productivity occur because the sum of the group effort is often greater than that of all the individuals. A group wisdom and a communal sense of sharing enlivens everyone working on the project. This does not mean that we do away with the traditional individualistic projects, but that they are counter-balanced with group activities.

Multi-Sensory Projects

If we have learned anything in the last fifty years about how children actually learn, it is that they all learn differently. The works of theorists from Jean Piaget and John Dewey to Howard Gardner and Reggio Emilia all confirm that each individual is a unique event, not just as reflected by our fingerprints or DNA composition, but in our particular way of grasping and perceiving the world and adapting to it. Consequently, the best educational and most sensible process would be one that accommodates and even capitalizes upon each individual's style of learning. This is, of course, nearly impossible in a system of mass education. In some cities today, the issue is the number of new schools that need to be built as fast as possible in which to cram burgeoning student populations. How we educate them appears not to be the issue. Yet, of course, it is the key issue, for continuing on the same path will simply guarantee another generation of angry, alienated, tuned-out and drop-out students.

Is it ever possible to allow for individual differences in a mass-education system? I believe it is, but only if we are willing to pay the price. To judge how each student best learns requires a substantial assessment process, small classes and highly trained teachers to recognize individual differences — teachers who can structure assignments and lessons consistent with those differences. All of this demands considerable funding.

Certainly, one way to accommodate individual learning styles is to recognize that certain students respond to and learn from particular sensory approaches. Some students respond well to auditory stimuli; lectures can work well with them. Others need visual access to the material. Others do well with projects they can physically construct. Certain students learn better when all three senses are brought into play. When multi-sensory projects are combined with cooperative-communal projects that involve a high degree of action and responsibility, then the level of *engagement* and excitement among the students is extraordinary. For educators, this peak teaching is most joyful and substantive.

Some bold schools are switching their evaluation procedures from only standardized testing to including portfolio assessments because portfolios allow for multi-sensory and cooperative projects; they allow students to show their individuality through diaries and journals, graphs and charts, art work, essays and term papers, poetry/creative writing, group reports and committee projects, self-evaluations and peer evaluations — all of which tell a fuller story than a single score. The process of assembling, reviewing, and sometimes presenting areas of these portfolios can be enlightening to the students and teachers. A test score is not a reflection of any part of a student's sense of self or accumulated knowledge. Rarely does a test score impart to a student a sense of purpose or meaning. It is a useful label which has utility value for such things as course grades and even college admission. It does not, however, fill the void that estranges so many students and which so few schools address.

Creative Self-Expression

It is a fundamental human need to express oneself: to say I am, I exist, I have something to offer to the world; I have a voice, a style of my own. This need will express itself one way or another. If it is bottled up, pressure will build and, like a shaken soda bottle, will pop and explode at some point. Students in over-crowded and under-programmed schools will also explode if they are denied positive avenues of self-expression. We can offer them drama in school theatre programs or watch them act out on the streets; we can provide arts classes or watch neighborhoods fill up with graffiti. It is useless to hope that adolescent energy will lie dormant and never burst free in wild and uncontrolled activity. Creative and expressive forms of dance, drama, music, visual arts and writing can channel this energy into positive forms, and even can help to transform entire schools and neighborhoods.

Somehow, the arts in America became relegated to a second-class curricular status — they are not considered core or "solids," they are classed as *extra*-curricular. This is a profound mistake, both practically and philosophically (See Chapter 10). Practically speaking, the arts contain an energetic quality, and through positive modes of self-expression, reduce negative modes. From the dawn of history, every civilization that has left traces provides proof of human beings' need to create, and to interpret through their creations their views of the meaning of life. For primitive societies, their drawings, monuments and sound-making *were* their curriculum. In ancient times the arts were always part of the "core curriculum." We are today one of the few cultures ever to think of the arts as *extra* to the curriculum. Life's values and meaning are most dramatically and profoundly captured by the arts. From *Antigone* to *Death of a Salesman,* to *Angels in America,* from cave paintings to Anselm Keifer, from Sappho to Adrienne Rich, we find representations of life's conflicts and glories, expressions that enable us to make sense of the chaos and conventions of existence. To dilute or delete such studies from our schools invites a host of negative energies to fill the void, ranging from collecting materialistic-consumerist trivia to anti-social behavior and violence.

When we place arts projects at the center of the curriculum, students come alive in ways that often amaze even the most hardened and cynical of adults. Students putting on a play or a dance or musical performance incorporate many of the other requisite sources: *books, action, responsibility, cooperation and communality, multi-sensory experience, creative self-expression* and *play*. They learn intellectually, they experience viscerally, and they gain meaning for a lifetime.

Play

Play is included primarily because life is brief, often filled with sorrow and dark times and ending, inevitably, in death. We can balance these grim realities with a lightness in play. The poet John Crowe Ransom (using the word "gay" in its older meaning of happiness) writes:

> Play sweeter than pray
> That the darkened be gay.

These lines hit me like a thunderbolt when I first read them. They come from Ransom's poem "Master's in the Garden Again" in which the master gardener — but really the poet-artist-everyman, "plays" in his dark, cold, and weed-filled garden trying to bring beauty and order to his piece of land.

For young people, and not just elementary age children, play is the way in which they apprehend the world. It demonstrates how they feel about life at its fullest. When we give short-shrift to the arts and other avenues of play, we all but guarantee that students will feel deprived and frustrated even though they may not articulate why. But we should know that if access to the arts has been limited, a crucial way to find meaning in life has been squandered.

A friend of mine, the poet and teacher Peter Levitt, often tells his classes this story in the first class meeting. He draws a block and a circle. The block, he tells the students, contains the standardized knowledge, the material for tests, quizzes, SATs and the like, which schools want you to learn. The circle is you, the student. When the block-knowledge has been absorbed by the students, the educators are happy and you have become a blockhead. The trick, of course, is to play outside the block. To be aware of what society wants to force upon you, to play the game when you have to, but to realize that it is a game, and that it is someone else's game. Finally, the real trick is to learn how to invent your own games. When we help students down that path, education is at its best.

This chapter summarizes how I think we can help students find meaning in their day-to-day education. What that meaning might be is the subject of the rest of this book. It is clearly subjective, reflecting our own biases — political, cultural, and philosophical — but gathered from direct interaction with students for over forty years. The following chapters are somewhat random and perhaps even idiosyncratic, but my co-writer daughters and I believe they add up to a coherent vision of education.

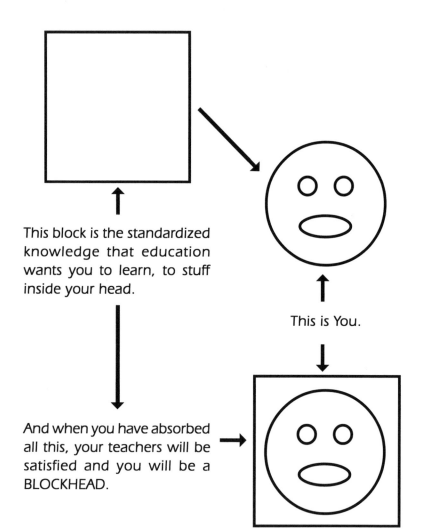

This block is the standardized knowledge that education wants you to learn, to stuff inside your head.

This is You.

And when you have absorbed all this, your teachers will be satisfied and you will be a BLOCKHEAD.

REFERENCES:

Buber, Martin. 1970. *I And Thou.* New York: Charles Scribner's Sons.

Dewey, John. 1938. *Experience and Education.* New York: Touchstone.

Levitt, Peter. 2003. *Fingerpainting on the Moon.* New York: Harmony Books.

May, Rollo, Ernest Angel & Henri F. Ellenberger, Eds. 1958. *Existence: A New Dimension in Psychiatry and Psychology.* New York: Basic Books.

Ransom, John Crowe. 1969. *Selected Poems.* New York: Alfred A. Knopf.

> *Pass by that which you do not love.*
> — Evan S. Connell

II

A NEW SOCIAL STUDIES

CHAPTER THREE

Meaning in Social Studies

No man is an Island, entire of itself; every man is a piece of the
Continent, a part of the main; if a clod were washed away by the sea,
Europe is the less, as well as if a promontory were, as well as if a manor
Of thy friends or of thine own were; any man's death diminishes me,
Because I am involved in Mankind; And therefore never send to know for
Whom the bells tolls' It tolls for thee.
— John Donne, *Meditation XVII*

What's the use of being timid? Why not reach out to the scruffy
grassroots . . . Life is so short. Why waste it just standing by?
— Ruth Conniff

Most likely we all remember pieces of our elementary school Social
Studies classes: making paper Indian chief headdresses, cutting out
models of the Nina, Pinta, and Santa Maria, building mini-pyramids
and the like. Our memories are usually connected with a sort of hot-
chocolate sense of nostalgia. Social Studies classes, in theory, are designed to acquaint children with diverse peoples and cultures, to imbue
them with a sense of respect for differences. In reality, I believe the
quaint process dilutes, distorts and even disregards the more crucial
elements of the subject. Too often the Columbus "discovery" myth over-
shadows the lesser-known history of the natives who already lived upon
the land. The building of the pyramids usually focuses upon architectural achievement rather than the misery, slavery, and mass death imposed upon the workers. The result is that real, underlying stories that
remain untold are lost opportunities for engaging young people in discussions about fairness, justice, slavery, dictatorship, and imperialism,
as well as exploitation.

I do not believe in depressing children in telling only horror stories
from the past. I do, however, believe that young people are quickly

interested by issues of substance. They generally want to know the truth, what the deeper issues were, and what relevance these stories have to the modern world. They are curious about historical events. The story of Columbus is a truly amazing story of navigation; it is also a devastating story of greed and racism. To neglect the latter is to deprive students of the potential for discovery. Racism and imperialism is an old story — a story that has continued into the 20th and 21st centuries. Social Studies is a subject where meaningful dialogue and debate should take place. Such dialogues would not only absorb students, but would make them more respectful of their teachers and classmates who think clearly. Teens often perceive school as just another adult establishment designed to keep things unchanged. Schools are usually not progressive forces for reform; too often they are obdurate agents of the status quo. For many young people today, however, the status quo is bankrupt. They find school boring. Society seems to offer little beyond materialistic consumerism — the shopping mall as Mecca. Schools do little to combat this empty message.

Schools should have three essential values at their core: a respect for diversity; a desire for social justice; and a commitment to preserving the earth's environment. The combination of these three would give teachers and students and, in fact, all of us, what we hunger for most deeply: a sense of purpose and definition in our lives. All three values are so inextricably linked that adhering to them or neglecting them may lead to survival or destruction. By highlighting these standards, teachers would impart to young people a sense that schools are not just passive purveyors of the mundane, but are participants in intelligent growth and sustainability. Voters stay home when the elections seem fruitless; similarly, many students don't attend school and even drop out when classes appear to be of no consequence. We must put substance into the educational process.

If Social Studies were to take a new tack, what might it look like? Here is a sample list of topics/courses:

1. The fate of indigenous peoples in the 20th and into the 21st century: imperialism and homogenization and extinction;

2. The Holocaust in Europe;

3. The population explosion;

4. Confronting our "past sins" — nations and their shadows;

5. Global economics: the growing disparities of wealth;

6. World poverty and hunger;

7. The role of social welfare in the USA today;

8. Economic growth and environmental degradation;

9. Racism: past and present;

10. Children's conditions and rights.

Each of these topics has the potential to involve students in important discussions and projects, and contains relevance to both their present and future world. Too often, aided by our current standardized-test tyranny, Social Studies and geography units wind up being lists of rivers, cities and countries to identify on maps. While identification and memorization of places is the end-all of machine-scored tests, the significance of these places is overlooked. To what degree are these rivers polluted? To what degree are the cities and countries experiencing deprivation, poverty, contamination, crime and corruption? To what degree are the inhabitants suffering from starvation, AIDS epidemics, industrialized economic exploitation, and civil, religious or international wars? These questions are rarely addressed by those who design the "national standards" we hear so much about. When politicians pontificate about accountability, too often they are advocating the regurgitation of facts and figures rather than expecting probing questions to stimulate discussion. Of course, they may not want to hold students accountable for knowing what they themselves are unwilling to account for. "National standards" in Social Studies does not mean an examination of our national sins and selfishness. In each of the ten topics I suggest above, the USA "standards" have been less than exemplary. Consequently, elected officials are not likely to suggest that our students explore those standards. This brings us back to the role of the teacher and the school's role in society. Is it to perpetuate the status quo or to encourage change in a dysfunctional world? Change will not come from the establishment, which by definition opposes change. So are schools simply servants of the establishment or should they try to effect change in society? Although they give lip service to the latter, in reality they are squarely in service to the former.

While my list is a suggestion of potential topics, let us examine approaches to teaching a few, and what their contents might include. I assume that these topics could be introduced and taught with age-appropriate exercises and activities from elementary grades through 12th grade. They are:

A. The Fate of Indigenous Peoples.

B. World Poverty and World Hunger;

C. Nations Confronting Their Own Past Sins — Their "Shadows" (covered in the next chapter)

A. The Fate of Indigenous Peoples

Wade Davis refers to the wondrous diversity of our planet as its *ethnosphere*, "a notion perhaps best defined as the sum total of all thoughts, beliefs, myths, and intuitions made manifest today by the myriad cultures of the world. The *ethnosphere* is humanity's greatest legacy. It is the product of our dreams, the embodiment of our hopes, the symbol of all that we are and all that we have created as a wildly inquisitive and astonishingly adaptive species" (Davis, 8). However, this magnificent diversity, perhaps our most critical human heritage on earth, is in jeopardy. Greed, racism and global technology, in the on-going context of colonialism and imperialism, continue to inflict devastation on indigenous peoples worldwide. There are perhaps 400–500 million indigenous peoples all over the world and they are being persecuted relentlessly. To give this number a quick comparison, it is equivalent to a world population greater than that of the United States. We ignore the ills inflicted on indigenous peoples because the media owned by the very global profiteers who indirectly or even directly benefit from "the system" do not cover tribal tragedies; the government seems almost oblivious to their fate; the ruling classes do not even put them on their radar screen. Businesses, banks and governments all over the globe threaten to destroy their future. Is this a loss to anyone but these unfortunate peoples? At least the questions should be asked. What better place than in schools from which our future leaders will emerge?

A worldwide tragedy of such major proportions demands attention in our schools. Not simply through random elective courses or graduate seminars, but as a concentrated, focused part of the curriculum in every school in the country. Where tribal peoples are not being murdered, they are losing the lands they have lived on for thousands of years. It's a lingering death. The bushmen of the Kalahari, Aborigines of Australia, Indians of the Amazon, reindeer herders of Siberia, all depend on the land for food, medicines, and identity with life itself. They are being flooded by dams, wiped out by disease, displaced by logging and mining, and evicted by settlers. All this is illegal; it benefits very few and is driven by greed and racism. It is also driven by the Western religion of "progress," adhered to unquestioningly and arrogantly.

Everyone loses in this process. Even the profiteers lose ultimately, for they destroy the very sources of profit for their own descendants. The biggest loser is humanity in all of its beautiful, rich and rapidly disappearing diversity. Globalization is an impressive sounding word, but too often it means profit for the few at the expense of the many and a numbing, dumbing-down homogenization of world culture. Social Studies classes can become museums of the past or serve as a forum where students are encouraged to actively debate the dynamic conditions of global diversity.

Consciousness precedes action. Students at all grades become active by first becoming conscious of the problems and issues. Once consciousness begins taking hold, students can engage in letter writing campaigns, food and book drives, sister-schools programs, fund raising drives, and other social-awareness projects. Consciousness must come first.

I envision, for example, a social studies course devoted to one single tribe. Perhaps a discussion of one tribe will illustrate how imperialism and exploitation of native peoples is not a phenomenon that only occurred 300–400 years ago, but continues today with equally devastating consequences. As a case, consider the Yanomami, "who inhabit the depths of the Amazonian tropical rainforests and whose lifestyle is based on an intimate knowledge of their environment and the ways in which they share its resources." There is a small book about the Yanomami published in the USA written by Paul Henley which gathers many sources and which would be an excellent book for children from 5th or 6th grades on up to 12th grade.

Indigenous people inhabited the Amazon Basin for over 10,000 years prior to its discovery by Europeans. Subsequently, colonization has reduced the native population from an estimated pre-contact population of five million to today's number of about 25 thousand people (with about 15,000 in Venezuela and 10,000 in Brazil).

The fate of the Yanomami was particularly compromised when gold miners began squatting on native land, assisted and protected by the military. The Yanomami have been branded as fierce and barbarous savages by the invaders, even though it is *their* land that is being invaded. Henley provides a balanced and unromanticized account of a tribe which is not a group of "noble savages," but simply human beings with strengths and frailties and with a complex and spiritual culture that he believes deserves to survive. He presents a culture with rich shamanic traditions, feasts and ceremonies, as well as a history of inter-village raiding with other tribes.

Nevertheless, other tribes pose no real threat to their survival. The threat has come from illegal small-time miners who have brought with them malaria, tuberculosis, influenza, and other respiratory disorders that the Yanomami lack immunity or medicines to combat. The miners have polluted the rivers with mercury, scared away game with their machines, and even massacred villagers. Between 1988 and 1990, as many as 1,500 Yanomami perished from disease and direct attacks.

A second book, *Murder in the Rainforest*, by Jan Rocha provides an in-depth but readable and specific account of how the Yanomami have suffered at the hands of economic progress, greed and globalization. Reading Henley and Rocha might supplant writing typical book reports about the Pyramids or memorizing the world's major rivers. In addition, the Lannan Cultural Freedom award winning photo-journalist, Claudia Andujar, has created a superb photographic book expressing the world of the Yanomami people.

A population greater than the United States, the world's 400–500 million indigenous peoples, are at risk. Meanwhile, in Social Studies classes, children all over the country learn about "the golden age of exploration" (a new video series for grades 5 and up), though it was clearly not so "golden" for the millions of indigenous peoples who perished as victims of European disease and murder.

The historical "age of discovery" is really a euphemism for colonization, imperialism, and exploitation not unlike the cultural genocide occurring in our own generation. We do not teach this in our schools except in the context of new euphemisms such as globalization or the free market process. It yields the same net results for poor, indigenous peoples: they lose their land, their culture, and, in many instances, their lives.

By studying effects of one commercial interest upon a specific native population, our students today will learn far more than by studying only the cultures of ancient civilizations, i.e., the Egyptians and the Pharaohs, lost kingdoms of the Mayans, or peoples of the Iron Age, the normal fare of Social Studies classes. Instead of a dependency on learning the names and dates of conquests and conquerors, we can have our students study the slavery and exploitation that existed then. Then we can point out that there are equally valuable cultures dying before our very eyes. As economic interests in the name of "technological progress" threaten to build dams, chop down forests and build roads into previously undisturbed eco-systems and interdependent tribal communities, we can see that the accumulated histories of ancient, diverse societies are endangered in a few short decades. One has only to read a single issue of *Cultural Survival Quarterly* or *Native Americans Journal* to see the daily attacks native activists are trying to repel. Any one of these issues would make for a challenging Social Studies unit, semester or year course. For example, take just the fall 2000 issue of *Cultural Survival Quarterly*. The issues it presents include: 1) The indigenous peoples of Burma whose plight is obscured by the civil wars occurring there. Every year, hundreds are killed, tens of thousands displaced, and the livelihoods of many more displaced by the Burmese army. Why? Which cultures are under assault? What do they believe? What are their rights? Their resources? What can the Western world do? What *is* it doing? These questions can be applied to tribe after tribe; 2) The struggle for citizenship and land rights by tribal people in Northern Thailand; 3) Indigenous peoples in Bolivia undertake protest march; 4) Brazilian development threatens Awá Indians; 5) Indigenous people of North

Russia — will they survive the 21ˢᵗ century? and 6) Taigana — the last reindeer herders of Mongolia — a documentary film.

Of course, the primary reason for designing Social Studies units and classes around the theme of preserving indigenous peoples is to cultivate values (and ethics of the acceptance) of pluralism, to raise consciousness of the relationship between genocide and ecocide, and to promote the respect of all living creatures. The value of cultural pluralism may seem self-evident, yet it is being undermined by the arrogance of those who assume that their dominant might equates with right. It is at best an impoverished assumption, yet one the Western world has acted upon for centuries. We cannot expect the powerful to accept changes that would in any way diminish their power. Most of us do expect educators to adopt enlightened positions and not simply serve a bankrupt paradigm. We can expect educators to teach students about current injustices that are perpetrated upon others. Consciousness precedes action. School is a pivotal place for consciousness to begin.

B. World Poverty and World Hunger

There are enormous discrepancies of wealth all around the globe, creating unspeakable woes for the world's poor. The same principle applies for this topic: consciousness precedes action. Students cannot fully develop values like concern and compassion unless they are made aware of the conditions of the approximately 1.2 billion poor people in the world, roughly 1/5 of the world's population. According to a Population Communications International White Paper: "In the 20ᵗʰ Century, world population nearly doubled . . . [and] the populations of many developing countries are expected to double or even triple again by 2050" (PCI,1). The purpose of a unit, semester, or even year's course on this topic is not to depress students, but to enlighten them and to issue a call to arms. If we do not teach students to care, of what value is our education?

Now some may ask, "All right, I can give a statistical list of horrible conditions, but what then?" I would propose to have students enter into a dialogue about how such conditions have come about and what possible solutions they might propose. The very dialogue will lead to questions about the distribution of the world's resources and wealth. First, the unit of study would ask:

- Who are the world's poorest people?

- Where do they live?

- What are the conditions of their lives?

- Is the rate of world poverty increasing or decreasing?

- Is there poverty in industrial countries, such as the USA?

- Is the gap between rich and poor shrinking or widening? Why?

- What is the relationship between education and poverty?

These questions, and the attempt to find group answers, could occupy students for months. Subtopics such as geography, economics, culture and politics would all come into play; however, they would come into play not just as facts to memorize for tests, but as an organic part of dealing with dramatic, moral and contemporary ethical questions.

I have rarely found students uninterested in the fate of their counterparts around the world. When they learn that nearly forty million people a year die of hunger, many of them children, they are not only appalled, but they want to know more. When they learn that three or four children die of malnutrition and disease about every ten seconds, we have teachable moments, moments of high student attention.

We can go on to look at other issues. For example: 1. *The relation of poverty to population:* When a child born today reaches the age of 25, there will be two billion additional people fighting for air, water, food, space, housing, jobs, schooling, roads, sewers, farmland. 2. *The relationship of poverty to environmental degradation:* If poor people can survive only by further depleting the world's diminishing resources, what will be the fate of us all? What might be done to provide alternatives for the poor? And what is the responsibility and even self-interest of the industrialized and more well-to-do nations to share resources with the poor? 3. *What is the history and justification of the disparity of wealth around the world?* The United Nations released a report in 2000 showing that the 222 richest individuals' combined wealth equals that of one third (two billion) the world's population, and that the three leading billionaires had amassed more than the total GNP of all 43 nations categorized as "least developed."

How has such a world social system evolved? Is this not a fair and important question to study in Social Studies? If we wish for students to take their education seriously, then the schools, teachers, and classes must themselves be places of serious discussion and activity. When students witness and participate in the classroom of a passionate teacher who presents her material with a sense of crucial importance, then students listen, they think, and they become involved in the process. Social Studies can be a place where passion and meaningful dialogue ignite fires within the young.

Postscript:

During the pre-publication period of this book project, Red Hen Press asked several outside readers to evaluate the manuscript. Each had helpful suggestions and one asked a question which I had to ponder long and hard. "Why," this reviewer asked, "given Paul Cummins' background as an English teacher, did he focus on social studies, the environment, politics and the arts, but not on English?"

I think the answer is that initially I was so focused on what is missing in many text-book driven social studies courses or on what is missing altogether from so many schools' curricula, i.e., the environment, the arts and politics, that I simply overlooked my own primary area of teaching experience. So let me address that initial oversight.

I believe the teaching of English, like so many other areas, is also endangered by an over-emphasis on preparing for standardized tests and by consciously or unconsciously avoiding controversial topics — the very topics which often engage students most. Themes of social justice can certainly be taught in reading pre-twentieth century literature, but often finding such connections are a stretch and do not immediately capture the students' attention. Class conflict can be gleaned from Dickens or Swift, but, in addition, why not go directly to a terrain and context more familiar to the students? Thus, if a given school were to follow our suggestions of teaching current social conditions in a social studies class, then the English teachers might simultaneously teach non-fiction works by a Carl Upchurch, Jimmy Santiago Baca, Luis Rodriguez, Dee Brown, Arundhati Roy, and the like. Or they might, for example, offer novels by Chinua Achebe, Fae Ng, Leslie Marmon Silko, Sandra Cisneros, and others.

And if humanities, civics, social studies and history classes were to consider the shadow side of American and world history, then English classes could enrich these courses, for example, with the poetry of protest. To this end, Carolyn Forche's superb anthology *Against Forgetting: Twentieth Century Poetry of Witness* is an invaluable resource. Many of the poems in this book provide students not just with the facts of genocide, revolution, and repression, but also — as is the essence of poetry — with the visceral experience of these topics. In my own teaching experience, for example, I found few students who had not become immediately absorbed by poems such as Denise Levertov's "Weeping Woman" or Paul Celan's "Death Fugue" or Bruce Weigl's "The Way of Tet." The poems in this anthology, as Forche writes in her introduction, are each "a specific kind of event, a specific kind of trauma" (33). By adding 20th century poetry and fiction to the study of recent major historical events, we give emotional depth to these studies and engage our students at the level where life is truly lived.

So, in addition to teaching grammar and rhetoric, composition and style, classical and traditional literature, AP and SAT test-taking skills, I believe the most important challenge for English teachers is to engage students at the experiential level by confronting them with the most serious issues of our times and with the concomitant essential challenges of the human condition.

REFERENCES:

Andujar, Claudia. 1988. *Yanomani.* Curtiba: DBA.

Davis, Wade. 1966. *One River: Explorations and Discoveries in the Amazon Rain Forest.* New York: Touchstone.

Forché, Carolyn. 1993. *Against Forgetting: Twentieth Century Poetry of Witness.* New York: W.W. Norton & Company.

Henley, Paul. 1995. *Yanomami: Masters of the Spirit World.* San Francisco: Chronicle Books.

Rocha, Jan. 1999. *Murder in the Rainforest: The Yanomami, the Gold Miners and the Amazon.* London: The Latin American Bureau.

Population Communications International. 2002. "The Impact of Population Growth: A White Paper." <http://www.population.org/resources/whitepaper.htm>.

> *. . . Myth is the secret opening through which the inexhaustible energies of the cosmos pour into human cultural manifestation.*
> — Joseph Campbell

CHAPTER FOUR

Social Welfare at the Core

Emily Cummins

She could not have dreamed but tiny dreams
Comparing them to yours . . .
— Robert Chambers

We can now recognize that the fate of the soul is the fate of the
social order; that if the spirit within us withers, so too will all the
world we build about us.
— Theodore Rosak, *Where the Waterland Ends*

As a first year graduate student (Masters in Social Work), I attended a series of seminars or modules relating to the various social problems one may encounter in any urban setting. I remember driving home after about the third module (and roughly three months of class and field work) in tears, processing the day while questioning myself: "Am I cut out for this? How is it possible not to "take it home?" when something within began to change. I felt frustrated. "Why," I kept asking myself, "are these emotionally charged, life changing field trips organized and reserved for those who already are committed to social service?" This question haunted me. After all, the professionals were preaching to the proverbial choir.

The following month, during a field seminar at the Los Angeles Public Council, a non-profit organization dedicated to helping welfare recipients, I realized that others shared my frustrations. After listening to a presentation outlining many staggering statistics of the public welfare system, a fellow student shouted out, "You know, I don't know why you're telling *us* all this, it's really my daughter's sorority that should be here!" After the laughter subsided, I shook my head once again over the ironic message. It's true, and she's right. The graduate students hearing this lecture and spending the afternoon amidst the chaos of the welfare system are, on some level, aware and concerned citizens. I mused upon how the message might reach those who lack awareness and exposure. It occured to me that these conditions, in connection with my own experiences and the experiences of others, might form the basis of a K–12 social studies curriculum.

Statistics and mainstream media are seldom a substitute for human interaction and social connection. I can compare formal education to personal experience and easily determine the more powerful of the two. As an undergraduate at Northwestern University, I attended a Freshman Seminar on the study of social problems. While I still own the books *Growing Up Poor, The Other America* and others, I remember little of the class. The professor, content, other students, none of it stuck. I can, however, recall vivid details from middle and high school community service outings. It would be equally impossible to forget countless specific faces, colored textiles, and exact words exchanged with children I encountered while traveling as a post grad throughout rural South America. These indelible images alter my perception, both of the social problems that lie within modern society as well as personal obligation to confront them.

In *Education and Social Problems* (1971), Carl Weinberg describes a form of education he calls "the humanistic school" while exploring a variety of societal predictions, social change, and the need for educational reform:

> The humanistic school will be concerned with knowledge, interpersonal relations, human potentialities, and social problems. Students will have an opportunity to be involved with all parts of their humanity in effecting change within the school and within the society (1971).

Weinberg preached that to continue education from the traditional perspective of "test and reward" while reserving the humanistic schools for those already enrolled, we must be prepared to acknowledge our shared responsibility in the rapid growth of social problems. As an alternative, consider what might happen if we began to integrate issues of social relevance, such as poverty and juvenile justice, into the elementary through the high school curriculum.

I had the rare opportunity in 2001 to witness the effects of education and field exposure on a select class of social welfare students. I met this handful of students when they enrolled in UCLA's Master in Social Work program after earning livelihoods in alternate fields such as law, business, and marketing. They explained that certain values and social significance seemed to be somehow lacking in their previous careers. I also watched another group of students enter the program announcing specific majors and concentrations only to find, usually through field experience, that their passions lay elsewhere.

Without some form of education or exposure, how will those who are sheltered, alienated, or perpetually distracted by mainstream patterns ever going to comprehend the necessity of resolving our social issues? This is not to imply that we should push all our youth into careers as public servants or social workers, for each individual must choose a separate path. Yet social and environmental issues are multiplying at a faster rate than we are able to handle, and we rely upon education and awareness to direct each person's path to include some form, whether through conventional or more creative means, of shared responsibility, communal effort and contribution.

So how can this be done? As with many visions, raising social consciousness requires a strong belief in the cause, focused commitment, and creativity. Instead of waiting for *someone else* or blaming the elusive "them" to take the lead in the fight for equality and social justice, we must focus our efforts within the classroom. Our political leaders continuously call public attention to the "younger generation" as the answer to many of our social ills, declaring education the magical solution. In order to substantiate this claim, we must design and implement curricula that will provide the tools to address our social challenges while instituting change.

Juvenile Justice
Inside the Walls

I wonder how many adolescents (or adults for that matter) have visited, or are familiar with, the structure of a juvenile detention center? I also wonder about the public misconceptions regarding what is being done to *rehabilitate* these youth. Surely there must be some form of counseling or direction, for how else do we expect children to break from the strongholds of poverty, racism, and systematized inequality? In addition to counseling, agencies must provide some type of individualized education plans for the inmates. And if nothing else, children must be required to complete minimal homework assignments; after all, they are just children.

While few detention centers provide rehabilitation, too often we find that they rely upon strict and punitive approaches within the current juvenile correction systems. Boot camps have become increasingly more popular, with focus on discipline, physical conditioning, and authoritarian controls as a means of curbing and controlling delinquent behavior. The popularity of such programs may be understood from the public perspective — they satisfy a general need to be proactive, appear to be "tough," are cost effective and focus on physical and mental structure. Few long-term studies on their impact however have been completed. One summary of existing evaluations reported little evidence of program effectiveness (Cullen, 1993) and theorists have criticized the potential for such models since they appear to abuse power and reinforce destructive images of masculine aggression (Morash & Rucker, 1990; Parent, 1989).

The Coalition for Juvenile Justice sums up the problem of the current juvenile justice system in the following statement:

> The majority of delinquents, even those who have committed serious crimes, will be released back into their communities [while they are still] in their teens and twenties. Without an education, without health care, without practical skills, without transition steps into their communities, without programs that have turned their antisocial activity into meaningful life lessons, what chance do they have of becoming productive law abiding citizens? What chance does our society have of becoming safe? (Mendel, 2001)

In spite of the concern voiced by professionals like these, we continue to support a programmatic approach that is failing to prepare targeted youth for a more positive lifestyle. Furthermore, in a society that already faces daily violence and crime, deficiencies in the care of incarcerated youth serve only to further threaten the well-being of our children, families, and communities.

As an alternative approach, we must provide youth with meaningful motivation and pertinent education to overcome the ingrained patterns of violence and destructive behavior. In addition, we can begin utilizing and exploring alternate approaches inside all classrooms. Lesson plans and units on social justice might inspire the youngsters early on who will one day become our future leaders and policy makers. We owe it to both the youth inside the detention walls as well as those outside to begin to consider our most pressing social issues, for how else can we expect to generate positive change?

Daniel Harr, an inmate who has written from inside the prison system in Wisconsin, explores the issue of educating inmates in his article "A Plea from Behind Bars: Take a Chance on Education." Harr, who has been criticized and even punished for his jail time writings, states that although education programs exist in certain prisons, "inmates find it nearly impossible to retain the positive aspects of such programs when constantly bombarded by such negativity." Prisons, he maintains, "are breeding grounds for the kinds of aggression and anger that teach life long lessons hard to unlearn for the majority of those who experience them." Harr, along with others, proposes that we target "education instead of incarceration" programs for offenders aged 18–25, offering specialized educational and career opportunities instead of what he calls the "school of rage and criminal thinking" currently employed behind bars. Similarly, Robert Gemignani from the U.S. Government Office of Social Responsibility observes, "For too long, education has been regarded as just another service for incarcerated youth. For too long, yesterday's pedagogy has failed to educate delinquent youth for today's world. It is time to change" (1994).

Theorists such as R. Hampton, P. Jenkins, and T. Gullotta, who research youth violence, make a similar claim. "To reduce youth violence, we must make a serious effort to provide young people with meaningful goals and roles in society and a sense that the future will offer them rewards for rejecting violence. When they have nothing to lose, too often violence seems acceptable." Harr and social theorists speak indirectly to methods and forces of prevention. If students in both regular and prison schools are engaged and learning about issues that directly affect their lives, they will feel a greater sense of purpose and worth.

Educational discussions on the outside could be designed from an adolescent perspective, based upon visiting and analyzing the conditions other adolescents face in detention centers. Additionally, students might devise and even participate in methods such as peer education. By doing so, children who live inside the walls are reminded that people on the outside (in this case, their peers) take interest in their future. Finally, pro-activity is modeled while teaching social responsibility, lessons which require guidance and repetition as much as core studies. Direct exposure could certainly find a place within the K–12 curriculum.

INTERRELATEDNESS — CONNECTING THE DOTS

Once we begin familiarizing our students with issues they are sure to confront outside their school halls, they are able to discuss methods of remediation that can be utilized within a social studies curriculum. Social problems do not exist within a vacuum, a reality that applies to most life relationships, from our relationships with one another to the earth we inhabit. Life is a seamless series of connections, links, and interchanges, each somehow altering the other. What better way to teach cause-and-effect than to consider how we influence one another, and as noted in chapters five and six, the effect we have on our planet.

Students might examine two separate social issues while focusing on ways they interrelate. By studying the history, social and demographic trends, as well as the policy behind two issues such as poverty and teen pregnancy, for instance, teenagers can be guided to explore the various links between the two. When students examine these concerns in the classroom, they may also discover that, while the problems are multi-faceted, the solutions are equally complex. Empowering lessons could be designed by having students study, explore, and propose solutions to the various issues they face in their own communities, as well as in the world at large. This might involve field trips to local political representatives, community agencies, shelters or foster homes, so that through a combination of experience and academics we may integrate additional messages: what happens to those around us *is* our problem and we have the power and strength to find solutions. There can be no more meaningful lessons for our youth to learn.

CONCLUSION
"Tell the Children"

I wish to revisit an experience and ultimate life lesson from my first year graduate studies. In one particular course, we were assigned the task of completing an in-depth community analysis in an area of our choice. My two partners and I selected Skid Row, Los Angeles, thus beginning our "assignment." Prior to the task, we had considered ourselves somewhat aware of what we might encounter in the upcoming months. In retrospect, we had no idea how profoundly this experience would affect us.

For the purpose of the project, we spent hours interviewing a variety of community representatives and discussing the various perspectives for our analysis. We spoke to a handful of agency workers who struggle daily to hold this community together. We felt and ultimately shared the fear and despair, especially from the women, the Skid Row population that most often goes ignored and underserved. I remember many of the voices, and I remember the faces of both residents and workers alike. There is, however, one voice that rose above the rest, an indelible reminder of the responsibility we all share in the battle for human justice.

His voice, soft and gentle, haunts me from time to time. This man, Robert Chambers, is one of the select few Skid Row residents who has "made it" and *has not* deserted those he left behind. Rather, he channels his community influence and presence through his work as the founder of "The Homeless Writers Coalition." Chambers, whose mere existence and survival breathes hope into this deprived community, turns to poetry and writing as his source of inspiration and expression as he does what he can for his "brothers and sisters."

The following is one of his poems, "Tiny Dreams":

> She could not have dreamed but tiny dreams
> Comparing them to yours
> For to live and have so little
> To live for so little
> To live on so little
> To compromise Death

Proceed with Passion

To compensate Life
The dream must be small
Sometimes the dream must be warmed food
A cold drink
A cup of water
A warm bubble bath
A white starched hanky
A dress
 A whiff of perfume
A flower in a vase
A spring night
A soft sod
A piece of dry cardboard
A pile of clean rags
Or rest when she was tired
Or dreams of rest
Of sleep
Of when the twilight of sleep
In the moment when fatigue and exhaustion mesh
The mending limbs surrender
And worry and fear flee
And nothing matters
No fear of flying
And all retreats into peace of dreams
Dreams
And kisses of angels
Dream of Dreams
Having given over to the Demons
The Big Dreams
The Big Dreams we take for granted
Tiny dreams availed her peacefulness
Of cool shade and bright shadow
Of new things
Of nurturing children in her arms
And cooking from the pantry
Sometimes of a sweet and tender loving man to protect her
Of singing in the Sunday choir
But the Demons had tricked her
These little dreams weren't Big Dreams at all.

The last time I met with Mr. Chambers, I concluded the session the way I often did, by exploring what can be done: "In your opinion Mr. Chambers," I asked, "where can, and where should we turn to institute positive change? Where do you think we might focus our efforts?" He listened intently, then swiveled his chair to face the window, rested his forehead momentarily on the glass and stared down the many flights to his "brothers and sisters" in the streets below. After a few moments of silence he spun around and replied, "Ms. Cummins . . . *tell the children.*" He paused again and then continued. "You see . . . I was there, pointing downwards, not too long ago. The adults, they walk on by, back and forth, back and forth, too busy with their lives to be bothered. But it's the kids, the kids will look, and they're not staring Ms. Cummins, believe me. I know the difference. They ask questions like, 'why do you sleep in that box?' or, 'why aren't you wearing your shoes today?' So, you see, we've got to tell the children. We got to keep tellin' em, and we got to tell them *why*, before they get used to not knowing, and used to not caring."

References:

Cullen, F. Nov. 1993. Control In The Community: The Limits of Reform. Paper presented at the International Association of Research and Community Alternatives Conference. Philadelphia.

Gemignani, R.J. 1994. Juvenile Correctional Education: A Time for Change. OJJDP Update on Research (Washington D.C.: Office of Juvenile Justice and Delinquency Prevention.

Harr, Daniel. 1999. "A Plea from Behind Bars: Take a Chance on Education." *Social Policy* Fall, 50–54.

Mendel, R. A. 2001. *Less Cost, More Safety: Guiding Lights for Reform in Juvenile Justice*. Washington, D.C.: American Youth Policy Forum.

Morash, M., & Rucker, L. 1990. A Critical Look at the Idea of Boot Camp as Correctional Reform. Crime and Delinquency, 36, 204–222.

Weinberg, Carl. 1971. *Education and Social Problems*. New York: The Free Press.

> *I don't know about you but I've been looking for a narrative in which suffering makes sense.*
> — April Bernard

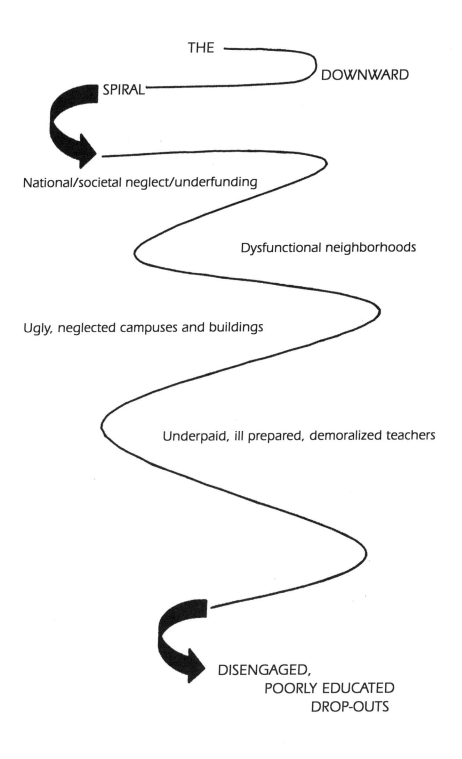

III

THE ENVIRONMENT

In the end we only conserve
*   what we love;*
We will only love what we understand;
We will only understand
*   What we are taught.*

— Baba Dioum, Sengalese Poet

CHAPTER FIVE

Learning for the Earth's Sake — And Ours

Anna Cummins

Education is no guarantee of decency, prudence, or wisdom. More of the same kind of education will only compound our problems. This is not an argument for ignorance but rather a statement that the worth of education must now be measured against the standards of decency and human survival — the issues now looming so large before us in the twenty-first century. It is not education, but education of a certain kind that will save us.
— David Orr, *Earth in Mind*

Returning to Los Angeles after a year in Europe, I found myself in a rather deep funk over the state of the environment and my contribution to it. Through reading and observation, this 23 year old had just begun to learn about the devastating ecological impacts of everyday life in an urban matrix, from our food choices, to our modes of transportation and consumption patterns, to something as seemingly innocuous as a daily cup of coffee. Reentry into the vast urban sprawl of a highly polluting city overwhelmed me, with a reminder at every turn that each of us is a small, albeit reluctant, cog in a tremendous, destructive mechanism. It left me feeling hopeless, powerless, and lost.

Despite gentle reminders from others that hope, not cynicism, inspires us to pursue productive change, a person of my generation could hardly *not* feel cynical, surrounded by daily warnings that humanity seems to be on a steady downward ecological spiral. Though I tried to tread lightly, I became consumed by the idea that simply by existing in today's society, I was in many ways contributing to our environmental degradation.

This personal struggle to maintain hope while inundated with visions of human ugliness and greed leads me to believe that education, or as suggested above, "education of a certain kind," is a critical antidote to the debilitating despair that continues to plague so many of us today. *Responsible* education can help us to better understand the changes happening around us, to understand how we have arrived at this point, and how much we have lost along the way.

To begin a discussion about environmental awareness with a litany of ecological grievances may be to replay the old record; however, it is important to keep in mind the magnitude of the issues facing us.

- In 2001, annual carbon emissions from fossil fuel combustion reached their highest levels in at least 420,000 years, probably in 20 million years.

- Primary tropical forests are disappearing at an annual rate probably exceeding 140,000 square kilometers — an area nearly the size of Nepal.

- Most of the world's coral reefs have been killed, damaged, or are in serious jeopardy due to overfishing, pollution, epidemic disease, and rising sea temperatures.

- 90 percent of the large fish (tuna, marlin, swordfish, etc.) are gone from our oceans.

- Plastic particles have been found to outnumber plankton in marine environments by ratios as high as 6 to 1.

- Lack of clean water or sanitation leads to 1.7 million deaths each year — 90 percent of them children.

The list of environmentally oriented imbalances continues indefinitely. Equally important to this discussion is a mention of the economic and social factors that contribute to environmental decline:

- The United States has the most unequal income distribution of all high-income nations, with over 30 percent of income in the hands of the richest 10 percent and only 1.8 percent going to the poorest 10 percent.

- In 2001 the average annual pay of U.S. CEOs topped $11 million — some 350 times as much as the average U.S. factory worker (who earned on average $31,260).

That our earth's beautiful, irreplaceable wilderness and many of its voice-less inhabitants have been under persistent attack from human igno-rance and corporate greed is certainly tragic. The deeper tragedy is that we still don't seem to care, despite generations of activism, and irrefut-able evidence of environmental decline. Most of us are aware, at least on some basic level, that something is terribly wrong with our relation-ship to on the planet. Yet we remain both shockingly ignorant and uninterested in the most basic ecological principles. Particularly in the North, where our resource-intensive lifestyles are responsible for a dis-proportionate amount of the damage, the implications of our educa-tional shortcomings transcend national and temporal boundaries.

While significant strides have been taken in the field of environ-mental education, we still remain in the infant stages of accomplishing what needs to be done. Much of what we call "environmental educa-tion" is for the most part an afterthought, a superficial inclusion to an existing educational framework that ultimately perpetuates our flawed, inequitable system. To truly get at the heart of our environmental crisis, we must come up with new, creative approaches that dare venture be-yond the traditional model. We must begin asking ourselves some pos-sibly uncomfortable questions about our roles and responsibilities in promoting healthier communities. And we *must* place the concept of "environment" at the center of our educational curriculum.

Education for What?

In *Earth in Mind*, a profound exploration of the need for educational reform, educational visionary David Orr echoes the question originally proposed by Aldo Leopold: "What is education for?" If education fails to inspire our respect and understanding for the extraordinary natural world that we depend on for survival, and encourages us to pursue lifestyles that revolve around the systematic degradation of our natural surroundings, of what possible use is it to us in the long run? What exactly does school prepare us *for*? What skills will be useful, and what will we absolutely need to know in upcoming decades? Researching answers to these basic questions, rather than faithfully adhering to stan-dard and perhaps outdated curricula, *should* provide the core for our educational systems.

This is not to suggest that we should abandon all conventional education, rather that the dilemmas to be faced by current and future generations are quite different from those of past generations. To attain more "sustainable" societies, our educational approach must evolve to fit the needs of a rapidly changing reality, one of exponential growth in a world of finite resources. Orr suggests "that no student graduate from any educational institution without a basic comprehension of the following:

- The laws of thermodynamics

- The basic principles of ecology

- Carrying capacity

- Energetics

- Least cost, end use analysis

- Limits of technology

- Appropriate scale

- Sustainable agriculture and forestry

- Steady-state economics, and

- Environmental ethics."

Clearly this list is targeted for a university audience. The idea holds, nonetheless, that students should leave school with a better understanding of the dynamics contributing to environmental impoverishment, and their own capacity to effect change. To this list, I would also add: principles of environmental justice, the relationships between poverty, gender, and environment, and the social, political, and economic history of environmental decline.

In addition to increasing students' environmental awareness, there may also be academic benefits to environmentally focused education. Centering curricula on local environmental issues may in fact increase students' interest in school, and improve their overall academic performance. To understand why this might be true, let's examine the concept of "environmental education," which means more than simply teaching children about whales and recycling. Comprehensive environmental education involves the use of pedagogical methods designed to train students in critical thinking and problem solving, to comprehend systems, to value and respect life, and to develop greater self-awareness.

What is Environmental Education?

According to the Belgrade charter, guidelines adopted in 1975 by the United Nations Educational, Scientific and Cultural Organization:

> The goal of environmental education is to develop a world population that is aware of, and concerned about, the environment and its associated problems, and which has the knowledge, skills, attitudes, motivations, and commitment to work individually and collectively toward solutions of current problems and the prevention of new ones.

To prepare students to comprehend the complexity of environmental issues, educators have developed teaching methodologies that cultivate an understanding of systems, cycles, and interdependence, as well as skills of critical thinking and problem solving. Environmental problems are enormously complex, caused by myriad factors including overpopulation, global poverty, corporate hegemony, large-scale commercial agriculture, racial inequality, third world debt, female literacy rates, fossil fuel dependent economies, and so on. Without some comprehension of how these individual pieces affect the whole, it is nearly impossible to make changes that restore, rather than further upset the ecological balance. And without grasping the complexity of environmental decline, the best we can hope for are simple solutions that do not, ultimately, address the root causes of our problems.

Our traditional educational model offers students separate disciplines of math, science, humanities, language, and (hopefully) arts, yet rarely encourages them to explore how these subjects interact with one another or with the world around them. This approach offers students a chance to glimpse only pieces of the whole picture. And then we wonder why they become frustrated, disengaged, and disheartened.

An integrated environmental curriculum on the other hand, one that centers around an understanding and concern for the environment we live, work, and play in, spans various academic disciplines by nature of the topic. Students covering a unit on energy consumption, for example, through conducting an energy audit of their school, develop skills in mathematics, economics, and science. Perhaps they will synthesize their findings in written reports, and may present these to the school administration or community, learning critical skills in both writing and public speaking. They might compare typical energy use in their school to that in other parts of the world, developing an understanding of the relative disparities in global consumption. Such a project could even lead to changes in the schools' energy practices, resulting in reduced energy costs for the school, and a sense of empowerment for the participating students.

As the above example illustrates, the skills developed by an integrated environmental curriculum are not limited to ecosystem issues per se. Rather, they are designed to cultivate a sophisticated worldview, one in which students learn to recognize, collect, and interpret relevant information, analyze problems, formulate and implement effective solutions, and evaluate results. The hands-on approach central to environmental education encourages students to develop skills individually and in teams, learning valuable lessons about personal motivation and cooperation with others. Guided to understand the relevancy and importance of their observations, students are *excited* to explore innovative approaches towards complex problems.

Academic Benefits: Engaging Students in the Process

Hypothesizing that students who participate in environmental learning programs respond positively across the board, educators and researchers from across the nation conducted an in-depth study on the academic impacts of integrated environmental education. (*Closing the Achievement Gap: Using the environment as an integrating context for learning.*) Results from this study suggest a positive correlation between **EIC** methods (using the Environment as an Integrating Context) and academic engagement:

"The observed benefits of EIC programs are both broad ranging and encouraging. They include:

- ◆ Better performance on standardized measures of academic achievement in reading, writing, math, science, and social studies;

- ◆ Reduced discipline and classroom management problems;

- ◆ Increased engagement and enthusiasm for learning; and,

- ◆ Greater pride and ownership in accomplishments."

Why should environmental study impact students' performance in other disciplines? As the title of this book suggests, students become disengaged from their studies when they fail to see the relevancy upon their lives. Conversely, when there is a logical purpose to subject matter, students are more likely to become active participants in their own education. Is not the primary complaint of students bored with school, "Why do I have to know this? What does it have to do with my life?" Haven't we all felt the same frustration with school at one time or another? And indeed, isn't the ultimate goal for all of us to find meaning in our lives, to feel that our time is spent in constructive, enriching pursuits with some tangible contribution to our immediate surroundings? When students, when we, find an understandable purpose to what we are doing, we are much more likely to thrive, flourish, and excel. This is what we live for.

It is difficult to imagine a topic more relevant or tangible to students than a study of their neighborhood, their city, their community and associated environmental issues. By designing the curriculum around a study of our immediate environment, studying ways in which our lives affect and are affected by the world around us, the question: "Why does this matter?" is answered before it is even asked.

Yet, according to a recent national survey of K–12 teachers, the number one reason given by those who choose not to teach environmental education (48.8%) was "lack of relevancy to their curriculum." How is it possible, I wonder, that a concept as all encompassing as "environment" cannot be made relevant to the academic subjects taught in schools? If we are taught, implicitly, that environment exists as an "other," unconnected to our daily lives, it is no wonder that we consider it irrelevant to our traditional curriculum.

Certainly, one obstacle to improved environmental education is a shortage of qualified, trained teachers. It is something of a catch 22: until we begin educating students today with greater environmental awareness, we will continue to produce generations of teachers who are equally unaware, and who in turn teach only what they have been taught. We must develop better resources, training programs, and workshops for teachers themselves. To demand of teachers that they somehow incorporate environmental issues into their curricula without adequate support or training is unrealistic. In my own experience as a first year teacher, I learned what a tremendous job preparing lessons, gathering materials, and trying to construct "educational yet entertaining" lessons is, without having an outsider telling me to somehow weave a given issue into my curriculum.

Difficulties in meeting already stringent state education requirements are often cited as a further obstacle for teachers in introducing environmental studies into the curriculum. The two, however, need not be mutually exclusive; in fact certain state requirements may actually mandate a degree of environmental education, For example, from the California state education requirements for 9–12 science, students should know:

- How to solve problems involving conservation of energy in simple systems with various sources of potential energy;

- How to analyze changes in an ecosystem resulting from changes in climate, human activity, introduction of non-native species, or changes in population size;

- That biodiversity is the sum total of different kinds of organisms and is affected by alterations of habitats;

- That a vital part of an ecosystem is the stability of its producers and decomposers;

- That a great diversity of species affects the chances that at least some organisms survive major changes in the environment.

A particularly unfortunate oversight in our educational mandates is the complete and utter lack of importance placed upon cultivating an understanding of our oceans. Marine conservation advocates nation-wide confront this difficulty in trying to promote better oceans aware-ness in schools. There are, as yet, no educational standards that require students to gain an understanding of the oceans; ecosystems that cover over 70 percent of our earth, regulate temperature and weather pat-terns, provide the major source of protein consumed by humans, pro-duce more oxygen than forests on land, and were the birthplace of life as we know it. The difficulties environmentalists face in promoting re-spect and understanding for the terrestrial earth, that which we can touch, smell, feel and, most importantly see, are magnified tenfold in trying to cultivate concern for what lies beneath our "anthro-myopic" line of vision. Few of us directly witness the damage we are inflicting upon our marine ecosystems, therefore it doesn't merit serious atten-tion, and is virtually absent from our educational agenda.

Clearly there are other, more pragmatic obstacles, such as funding — ultimately a question of national priorities. Sooner or later, we *will* pay for today's omissions, just as we are now paying for yesterday's. Environmental education is not an "extra-curricular" that we must some-how find the funds to squeeze in, it is critical to every aspect of our long-term survival.

As Orr notes in *Earth in Mind,* "All education is environmental education," either by inclusion or omission. By omission, we teach that the environment is not important enough to be included in curricula along with more "substantial" academic disciplines. By *not* teaching about renewable resources and the need to conserve, we teach that the world is an infinite source of materials waiting to be consumed. By *not* educating students to understand systems, we perpetuate the ideology that we are isolated beings, separate both from nature and from our collective impact upon it.

These lessons are learned young. Yet we begin life as little environ-mentalists, drawn to the outdoors before we even understand why. A creek, for example — a tiny ecosystem in microcosm — presents an endlessly fascinating playground for a child, providing hands on les-sons in life cycles, biodiversity, geology, biology, and many other sub-ject areas. How many of us have strong childhood memories of playing, enraptured, in the outdoors? Whether nature was a weedy clump of grass flourishing in an abandoned city lot, a storm-water fed urban stream hosting tadpoles and moss, or vast meadows, beaches, and unspoiled forests, the impulse and the experience stem from the same place. We gravitate towards the outdoors as children, but are later distracted from this early passion by more pressing concerns of school, work, career, or simply surviving.

For many of us, the doubts, confusions, and headaches of our mechanized urban lives evaporate in the presence of natural beauty; absorbed by alpine air; diminished by the humbling reminder of our profound smallness. Perhaps our day-to-day focus would become a little less distracted, a little more meaningful if we were taught to preserve, rather than destroy, our childhood playground.

Despite having painted a rather bleak, discouraging picture of our antiquated educational system, we actually are seeing extremely positive improvements in environmental education. More and more schools are beginning to offer some form of environmental studies, networks of communication between schools and educators are improving, research institutions are investigating both the need for and the benefits of environmentally based curricula, and resources are becoming more accessible. These are still however the exception. Many obstacles bar the road to more widespread adoption of environmental principles. We believe that these difficulties will lessen as current efforts prevail, and as students become engaged in dialogues concerning environmental sensitivity.

REFERENCES

Leopold, Aldo. 1949. *A Sand County Almanac.* New York: Oxford University Press.

Lieberman, G., and L. Hoody. 1998. "Closing the Achievement Gap: Using the Environment as an Integrated Context for Learning. *State Education and Environment.*

Moore, C.J. et al. *2002.* "A comparison of Neustonic Plastics and Zooplankton Abundance in Southern California's Coastal Waters." *Marin Pollution Bulletin 44.*

Myers, R. and B. Worm. 2003. "Rapid Worldwide Depletion of Predatory Fish Communities." *Nature.*

"National Report on Environmental Attitudes, Knowledge and Behavior." 2000. Washington, *D.C. National Environmental Education and Training Foundation.*

North American Association of Environmental Education.<http://www.naaee.org>.

Orr, David. 1994. *Earth in Mind: On Educaton, Environment and the Human Prospect.* Washington, D.C.: Island Press.

Shifting Baselines. <http://www.shiftingbaselines.org>.

State of the World 2003: A Worldwatch Institute Report on Progress Towards a Sustainable Society. New York/London: Norton and Company.

"United Nations Belgrade Charter, Tbilisi Declaration." 1977. Intergovernmental Conference on Environmental Education.

> *The central question may soon become how much we think we want to learn about what hasn't been incinerated, lest more be monkeyed with; learning so often leads to monkeying.*
>
> — Edward Hoagland

CHAPTER SIX

The Campus as Classroom:
Green Building and the Learning Process

Anna Cummins

The problem is not just that many academic buildings are unsightly, do not work very well, or do not fit their place or region. The deeper problem is that academic buildings are not neutral, aseptic factors in the learning process . . . Academic architecture is a kind of crystallized pedagogy . . . buildings have their own hidden curriculum that teaches as effectively as any course taught in them. What lessons are taught by the way we design, build, and operate academic buildings?

— David Orr, *Earth in Mind*

The unifying theme throughout this book is students' lack of connection to their education: disengagement is manifested in high drop out and low attendance rates and a general academic malaise. Providing students with a true sense of ownership and connection to their education will require more than curricular reform; it will require changes in the way we view the school campus itself — the very classrooms, buildings, and communities in which learning takes place. These spaces speak volumes to the observant listener.

How and what can a classroom teach? Designed responsibly, a school's campus can teach students to respect and conserve natural resources, and to better appreciate their potential as environmental stewards. Designed intelligently, learning spaces can be made healthier, greener, and more vibrant, while saving schools thousands of dollars in energy costs. Designed, on the other hand, according to conventional building standards, school buildings teach just the opposite:

The extravagant use of energy in buildings . . . teaches students that energy is cheap and can be wasted. The use of materials that are toxic to manufacture, install or discard teaches carelessness about the use of Creation and a kind of mindlessness about where things come from and at what cost. Windowless rooms, or those with windows that do not open, teach that nature is to be kept at arms length (David Orr).

The notion that a building can teach and inspire is slowly gaining momentum in educational circles. A tour, however, of our nation's unimaginative scholastic barracks reminds us that we remain in the infancy of widespread reform. The following example paints a portrait of the evolution beginning to take place in schools across the nation, a portrait of what could and should be.

Snapshot: a day in the life of Lagoverde High

At the end of the 20th century, Lagoverde was much like any other school across the nation. Built in the 1940s, the campus was in great need of repair. Old roofs, windows and floors, inefficient heating and lighting systems, cracked asphalt and chipped paint all contributed to exorbitant energy costs and a faded façade. Encouraged by reports of potential savings in energy costs, the school's administrators decided to try incorporating "green building" techniques in the renovation process by replacing fossil fuel-dependent energy systems with solar power. Though some initially feared high upfront costs for equipment installation, estimated long-term savings of $271,900 per year helped to silence even the most resolute protestors.

As they watched their energy bills decline, Lagoverde administrators witnessed an equally valuable transformation take place in the student body. In the project's early stages, the school's planning commission had invited students to participate in the process along with teachers, contractors, and architects. Students were asked to voice their opinion on various campus features, and were engaged in discussions on the environmental and economic benefits of the school's new makeover. The results were thrilling. Students began to show a newfound interest and pride in their surroundings. For the first time, they felt included and respected — they were made to feel that their input mattered. Within a year, attendance rates doubled, dropouts declined, and test scores increased by 15%.

Encouraged by their success, students and teachers began seeking ways to further improve their schools' sustainability. They envisioned a "high performance" school, one that limits its negative impact on the surrounding community while enhancing the capacity of its occupants to learn and live. The following snapshot provides a glimpse of what they achieved, a living laboratory that nurtures, breathes, and most important, teaches students to hope.

7:45 a.m. The school parking lot, though bustling with morning traffic and somnambulant teens, seems more *park* than *lot,* a sort of urban forest in the midst of a concrete wasteland. Between each car space stands a leafy tree providing shade for cars parked beneath, planted by last year's green team. The trees reduce the amounts of pollutants emitted by cars exposed to direct sunlight, provide natural cooling, absorb carbon dioxide, and offer some visual respite from the neighborhood's otherwise industrial gray monotony. Small strips of greenery flecked with yellow flowers separate the rows, providing a much-improved alternative to blacktop. These floral rows, or "vegetated swales," reduce the amount of urban runoff that floods into storm drains carrying pollutants, oils and debris directly into major waterways during heavy rainfall. In place of standard asphalt, the parking lot is made of semi-porous pavement, allowing rainfall to seep into a large underground cistern that collects water to irrigate the playing fields. This conserves water, saves money, and further reduces toxic urban runoff. A colorful, interpretive sign produced by last year's 8th grade art class welcomes visitors to the school, and details the parking lot landscape. On either side of the placard stands a long row of bicycle racks, filling quickly by students participating in the "human power" bike club.

In the school's central courtyard, a group of 10th graders cluster around a pond before their first period class. The pond, host to tilapia, frogs, and millions of microscopic aquatic creatures, is an endless source of both fascination and pride for them, particularly because they helped design and build it during a biology unit on wetlands. The unit focused on wetlands' natural ability to purify water, a characteristic that students will later test in chemistry lab. Hyacinths float languidly on the pond's surface, filtering heavy metals and bacteria from the water, which they break down into naturally occurring substances.

Other students check eagerly on their vegetable garden. A rainbow of peppers, tomatoes, corn and radishes hang heavily from leafy plants, inspected daily by the solicitous teenagers. In addition to its fun factor, the organic garden has proven to be a valuable outdoor aid to complement lessons in plant reproduction, photosynthesis, nutrient recycling, water cycles, and a host of other topics related to food and agriculture. Students will carefully monitor the garden's progress throughout the year, testing soil acidity, graphing plant growth, and keeping watchful eyes for pests or diseases. Field trips to local nurseries and farmers' markets, guest speakers and parent volunteers helped to make the garden a truly cooperative effort, which they will celebrate after the first harvest with a community feast.

8:00 a.m. Students filter into brightly lit classrooms to prepare for today's lessons. Natural sunlight channeled through special solar tubes provides the classroom's warm, soothing light. This process, known as daylighting, saves the school close to $77,000 in energy costs and reduces greenhouse gas emissions by 1500 pounds a year. Additionally, studies show that daylighting contributes to improved overall health. Students attest to a noticeable lightness in the air; they feel somehow more productive, focused, and calm. If testing is any measure of productivity, this is supported by a 5–7% increase in test scores since harsh fluorescents were replaced with natural light.

The room is absent of neatly lined rows; instead, students gather in groups at small workstations. In one cluster, a group begins working on a project to study insulation. They are comparing the different capacities of insulating materials by building mini "insulators" using soda cans, fiberglass, wool, styrofoam, newspaper, and aluminum foil. Next, they will measure the temperature of water heated at various intervals in each can by incandescent lamps, recording the differences in heat loss over time. Certain materials more efficiently reduce heat loss in cold weather, and heat gain during hot weather. As a class, they draw the analogy between soda cans and buildings, and discuss the importance of proper insulation for energy conservation in their school and homes.

Another cluster finds students monitoring Lagoverde's solar power capacity. Through internet connection to a local energy company database, students are able to track the amount of solar energy produced by the school's photovoltaic system, and compare this to the total amount of energy being consumed by the buildings. Their assignment: to create a graph on the computer that depicts their results, which they will display on the school's "feature of the week" bulletin. This space provides a venue for students to post projects, papers, and artwork inspired by some aspect of their campus. The teacher strolls the room, checking in with individual group projects and answering questions, eventually calling the whole class together to share their findings.

In other classrooms around the school, traditional topics of math, science, social studies and English are made immediate, woven seamlessly into the environment of the school and greater community:

- A geometry class tours the campus, studying the importance right angles play in structural foundations;

- In a unit on the industrial revolution, students study the history and impacts of fossil fuels, making it relevant by examining the types of fuel used in their school and homes;

- An earth sciences class sets out on a field trip to the local wastewater treatment plant, where they will create a map tracing the life cycle of their local drinking water, from source to treatment plant, to users, and beyond. They will travel, no less, in the school's vegetable-oil fueled bus.

These are just a few of the infinite learning possibilities presented by mindful, intelligent design. While Lagoverde High is a fictitious school, it draws upon real world examples of existing educational projects, and represents a timely trend in schools nationwide. More and more schools are realizing the tremendous educational, economic and environmental potential of designing high performance "green" campuses.

By the year 2007, we will need to construct 6,000 new schools. If these schools districts represent the average national profile, they will spend $110 per pupil annually on energy, approximately $6 billion overall. Much of this money, desperately needed for increased teacher salaries, arts and human development courses, smaller teacher to student ratios, books, materials etc. will be needlessly burned through inefficient, polluting energy systems. Schools *could* save 25% of that money, totaling $1.5 billion nationally, by investing in energy-efficient equipment, improving operations and maintenance, and supplementing energy consumption with renewable sources such as solar, wind or geothermal.

Beyond economic savings, though this alone should be sufficient incentive to a societal sector that is invariably the first to suffer during times of economic hardship, schools serve to benefit from numerous other components of green design, such as:

Increased on-campus learning opportunities
By involving students in the planning process, incorporating design features into lesson plans, and generating dialogue about the need to protect our resources, schools can transform their campuses into active, experiential learning laboratories. In doing so, they tacitly teach students about the connection between our lifestyles and the environment in a way that is proactive and hopeful rather than alarmist.

Improved health and academic performance
Numerous studies show that students in schools that utilize natural light (i.e. daylighting) perform better on tests by 5–15%. Additionally, the indoor air quality in buildings that eschew toxic, chemically processed materials in favor of natural, locally produced products is cleaner and healthier.

Reduced environmental impact
According to the Worldwatch Institute, building construction and renovation accounts for approximately 40% of our raw material use, 40% of landfilled materials, and 40% of our energy consumption. By improving energy efficiency, reducing waste, conserving water, and using non-toxic recycled materials, schools can reduce their "ecological footprint," their impact on planetary health.

> If all US public schools upgraded their space to meet energy-conservation standards, they would save nearly $733 million a year — and the reduction in air pollution would be equivalent to removing one million cars from the nation's highways (Alliance to Save Energy).

Finally, a truly green campus is one that creates a sense of community, that elicits input from future users, and that *educates* users about the resources needed for operation and maintenance. At its best, green building serves to *enhance* our experience by reminding us of our interconnectedness with our environment, rather than simply sealing us off the outdoors.

❖

Beyond what we learn from our teachers in school, we learn a tremendous amount from our surroundings. We are *complex* learners. We assimilate knowledge through all of our senses, especially in our youth, when with an insatiable appetite for new information, we devour our surroundings and formulate new conclusions on a daily basis. We are *diverse* learners. Some of us respond to words on a chalkboard, some to pictures and diagrams, others thrive outdoors and begin to fade if pent up inside for too long. Some learn by watching, others by doing. We should take every opportunity to celebrate our unique and wonderful learning capabilities, whether they be visual, physical, kinesthetic, logical, or interpersonal. By designing learning environments that teach, inspire, and stimulate curiosity, we give students opportunities to learn in multiple ways. Buildings that are efficient, that respect rather than destroy life, and that teach students to value energy and resources literally surround them with real, tangible symbols of hope.

Perhaps hope is the most valuable lesson students can learn from a green campus. Becoming cynical or apathetic about our future planetary prospects is no longer a rarity amongst young people. Visible threats to environmental health — and consequently our own — become every day a little less abstract, and a little more immediate. We are starved for positive messages.

As humans, we must believe in our capacity to improve our surroundings, albeit on a small scale. Few things provide us with more purpose, meaning, or satisfaction than the knowledge that our actions create ripples of change, and that we have some control over the quality of our communities. By surrounding young people every day with reminders that there are plausible, innovative and functional ways of meeting our daily needs, we teach them that there are alternatives to the status quo. When they in turn learn to challenge the tried, though not necessarily true, students begin to understand that the "less traveled" path may in fact be the most logical and harmonious. This might just make all the difference.

REFERENCES AND LINKS

Alliance to Save Energy: Green Schools Program
<http://www.ase.org/greenschools>. Includes lesson plans, curriculum
resources, classroom tips, and useful links.

American School Board Journal:
*Learning By Design 2000: A School Leader's Guide to Architectural
Services* <http://www.asbj.com/index.html> Annual Journal showcasing exemplary school design projects from across the continent.

High Performance Schools Act
In 1999 the House of Representatives created the High Performance
Schools Act. The purpose of this Act is to "assist school districts in the
production of high performance elementary and secondary buildings
that are healthful, productive, energy efficient, and environmentally
sound." More info at: <http://rs9.loc.gov/cgi-bin/query/z?c106:H.R.3143>

National Energy Education Development: <http://www.need.org>
Includes curriculum resources, state and local programs, and related
information.

Orr, David. 1994. *Earth in Mind: On Education, Environment, and the
Human Prospect.* Washington D.C.: Island Press, *Environmental
Building News*, Volume 11 # 2, Feb. 2002.

Plimpton, Patricia; Conway, Susan; and Epstein, Kyra.*Daylighting in
Schools: Improving Student Performance and Health at a Price Schools
Can Afford.* National Renewable Energy Library, Washington DC,
2000. <http://www.deptplanetearth.com/nrel_student_performance.htm>

US Department of Energy: Resources for Schools <http://
www.energy.gov/school/index.html>

> *"We need another world ," she says.
> Yes, but there is no other.*
> — Robert Coover
> *Stick Man*

IV

POLITICS AND EDUCATION

"... one nation, divisible, with liberty and justice for some."

CHAPTER SEVEN

The Political Dimension of Education

The cure for the evils of
democracy is more democracy.
— H.L. Mencken

The brave make a place at
their table for evil. For only first-hand
knowledge of evil can transform meditation
into action.

— *Ellen Hinsey*

The political dimension is often present in education, and by ignoring it we indirectly make a decision to support the existing system with all its inequities and indecencies. It is indecent to allow children to grow up in abject poverty, and to accept the fact that certain children are doomed by the accident of being born into poverty, homelessness and slums.

Schools participate in a political-economic system whether their occupants like it, acknowledge it, or not. We are not so naïve as to assume that the educational establishment would readily agree with this thesis and make any effort to change. Why? Because the system by its very nature must endorse the greater establishment of which it is a part. Most schools, along with the media and all levels of the government, exist to protect the oligarchy from any intrusion or change. As Gore Vidal writes: "The corporate grip on opinion in the United States is one of the wonders of the Western world. No First World country has ever managed to eliminate so entirely from its media all objectivity — much less dissent" (41).

Those few who control the media that exists to distract, entertain, and anesthetize the public, and who purchase the government through the auctions which we call elections, also indirectly control the schools. Many teachers and principals who work in our schools have themselves been inculcated into the existing social structures under the auspices of that media and political and educational establishments. As the old saying goes, you can't fix a problem at the level of the problem, and our problem is the society itself with its disparities of wealth and profound addictions to consumerism and trivial entertainment and to unbridled profiteering.

What is to be done? For a beginning, individual teachers, principals, and even school systems might pledge to at least take a closer look and then question whether they want to live in a world in which:

1. The leading economy (the USA) spends twelve times more on promoting arms sales abroad than on environmental technologies.

2. Two hundred twenty-two individuals in the world have wealth equal to one third (two billion) of the world's population.

And, if this is not the world we want to inhabit, then we ought to consider two responses: study and action.

Study

The study component would require a close look at global inequality and how it came about. It would include reading about controversial topics and asking tough questions. Here, I believe, we receive an immediate dividend: students will find the process meaningful. They will become absorbed in the process. Most young people have a basic and deep-seated sense of fairness. They react almost viscerally to unfairness. The reality of homeless people living literally in the shadows of new multi-million-dollar condominiums and concert halls captures their attention instantly. How can this be, they ask? Once they have asked the question, real education begins.

It is certainly appropriate to teach students how American democracy is supposed to work: the Constitution, the Bill of Rights, and the election process for starters. It is inappropriate, however, to leave off at the descriptive level and ignore the evaluative level. Yes, we hold elections. But is it fair that a small percentage of wealthy donors determine who can afford to run for office and determines their agenda and even to whom they shall be beholden once elected? Surely this is fair game for class discussion, and, ultimately, for action.

Thus, in addition to the traditional questions, such as: What are the three branches of government? and, How do checks and balances function? I would suggest a whole different genre of questions. Here are ten examples from a potentially longer list of questions:

1. Are elections for sale?

2. Do guns make us a safe society?

3. Does the global market benefit all people?

4. What is/what should be America's position regarding the fate of indigenous peoples?

5. What should be the United States' relationship to the World Court? The United Nations?

6. What should be the ratio between defense spending and education spending?

7. Why does the US allow between 16–20% of its children to live in poverty?

8. Why are there homeless people in the world's wealthiest nation?

9. Why are minority groups such a disproportionate population among all drug violators in prison?

10. Why do women receive less pay than men for the same jobs in America?

In addition to asking such impolite questions, we need also to confront other realities that students may recognize while schools gloss over them. Many students are aware of historical lies and are quickly disengaged when their "crap-detectors" are activated. Glossing over harsh realities, according to James W. Loewen, "can become something of a burden for students of color, children of working-class parents, girls who notice the dearth of female historical figures, or members of any group that has not achieved socioeconomic success. No wonder children of color are alienated" (3). To which I would add, it's no wonder that so many students are disengaged, alienated, and filled with a sense of the meaninglessness of their studies.

I do not propose teaching only doom and gloom courses, or courses that demonize the United States. Yet I do believe that students will take their education more seriously when they perceive that their teachers and schools are not simply serving bromides or unexamined fictions, but are courageously seeking the truth. This leads us back to my question: What are schools for? Paolo Friere offers an answer which I heartily endorse: "To think of history as possibility is to recognize education as possibility. It is to recognize that if education cannot do everything, it can achieve some things . . . One of our challenges as educators is to discover what historically is possible in the sense of contributing toward the transformation of the world" (40). Clearly, Friere believes that education must address my initial question, "what kind of a world do we want to inhabit?"

In the twenty-first century, this question inevitably leads us not only to politics, but to environmental concerns (which are usually political as well). For the very question raises not only quality of life issues, but to survival of species, languages, indigenous cultures, lakes, rivers, oceans, of the very air we breathe and food we ingest. Certainly, most schools pay attention to the current scientific-ecological matters. But few schools present the political dimensions of these issues. It is, I believe, unconscionable for schools to ignore the essence of the major threat to the survival of all species, human beings included. The threat is this: the world, our planet, cannot "sustain many more doublings of industrial output under the present system without experiencing a complete ecological catastrophe" (Danaher, 35). All the graduates of every elementary, high school and college in America should recognize this concept as the core of their education. It is not a Democratic or liberal, or Republican or conservative controversy, it is a human issue. By placing economic growth as the highest value, by measuring the health of the nation's resources only in economic terms, we are depleting the earth and our children's future. It is a political issue in that politicians who are servants of oligarchic profiteers will not tackle the issues. Consequently, if schools do not teach students that this is so, then who will?

Some of the questions raised by a study of politics and the environment might be:

1. Why is it that people of color in urban and rural areas are the most likely victims of industrial dumping, toxic landfills, uranium mining, and dangerous waste incinerators?

2. Why is it that the producers (national and multi-national corporations) who profit by the damage and depletion of the environment and its resources do not record such destruction as a cost of production? Why does clean-up and management of industrial and commercial waste and dumping become a cost of the state and its tax-payers?

3. Do we really wish to argue that the principle of endless accumulation of capital by fewer and fewer people transcends the principle of the preservation of the biosphere?

4. Should the government play the role of protector of free markets with minimal government restraints, or a role of strong intervention to ensure clear air and water, unpolluted food, and preservation of biodiversity?

Surely questions like these warrant serious attention in our schools. The failure to confront such issues guarantees that current trends become our destiny.

In addition to environmental studies, students must also be taught that there is a political dimension to the media. The media are owned by the very forces whose goal is to maintain their own power while remaining invisible to the public. Accordingly, the role of the media is to facilitate this process.

> Currently, the media limit political debate by the narrow range of stories they address and, even more importantly, by the limited range of voices and perspectives regularly featured as part of their coverage. As long as commentary and analysis of public affairs is provided by a narrow range of individuals representing powerful corporate and government interests, inclusive democratic debate that truly reflects the diversity of our society will not exist. Dissent and diversity will not be found, as long as access to the mainstream media is granted by invitation only (Croteau & Hoynes, 195).

Action

I stated earlier that students find meaning in their education when they are asked to confront substantive issues in their studies, especially when they are engaged in active projects. Action suggests that all is not lost, that the possibilities for change are there to be seized. Action is the enemy of passivity, boredom, and alienation. Of course, action is enormously difficult. The forces of the status quo will do everything they can to discourage student activism, whereas, I believe they should do just the opposite. If the schools really believed in the value of democracy, they would encourage students to participate, to make their views known, to march, to write letters to Congress, to hold student and city-wide conferences, to invite controversial speakers to their schools. The administration will rarely, if ever, sponsor such activities. It must come from the handful of teachers and students who see the political dimension of education. If it does not come from these brave souls, it is unlikely to come from anyone or anywhere.

At New Roads School in Santa Monica, California, we changed the name of one area of our curriculum from *Community Service* to *Community Action*. The idea is that whatever the students study — child labor, animal rights — that there also be an action component so that the students identify ideas as forces for social change. It almost doesn't matter which issue students choose to become involved in. What is crucial is the very process of involvement, or engagement. Thus, student clubs, with adult sponsors and guides, or action classes, might focus on any number of issues to include action experiences: civil rights, women's rights, children's rights, gay-lesbian rights, animal rights, or anti-nuclear, anti-arms races, peace movements, environmental protection, or any other consciousness raising topics. All are potentially valuable ways of enabling students to participate in the democratic process rather than being passive, despairing, or cynical audiences of the show.

To help students become active, we need to acquaint them with other activists who have launched grassroots movements. In an era where one politician after another is tarnished with scandal or partisan narrowness, young people need heroes. The schools need to bring these heroes into the curriculum, onto the campuses. Students need models. For example, they might consider the story of Julia Butterfly Hill, the author of *The Legacy of Luna: The Story of a Tree, a Woman, and the Struggle to Save the Redwoods*.

In an effort to prevent the corporate onslaught of Pacific Lumber Co. against the clear cutting of the majestic redwood trees in northern California, Julia lived in a platform atop one redwood tree for 738 days — just over two years. She endured physical hardships, terrifying storms, public and media ridicule, and deep personal hardships. She endured, however, and her courageous act of civil disobedience helped to not only save the Luna, one beautiful tree she inhabited, but to draw attention to the issues of sustainability and forest preservation, as well as forging an agreement with Pacific Lumber to preserve Luna and a buffer zone around her. It was a small victory in practical terms, but a major one symbolically. Julia Hill Butterfly became engaged in the process of learning. In her own words:

> Living in this tree, I remembered how to listen, to hear the world and Creation speak to me. I remembered how to feel the connection and conscious oneness that's buried deep inside each of us.
>
> So I will continue to stand for what I believe in, and I will continue to refuse to back down and go away. No person, no business, and no government has the right to destroy the gift of life. No one has the right to steal from the future in order to make a quick buck today. Enough is enough. It's time we as humans return to living only off the Earth's interest instead of drawing from the principal. And it's time we restored some of the capital investment that we've already stolen.
>
> Luna is only one tree. We will save her, but we will lose others. The more we stand up and demand change, though, the more things will improve. I ask myself sometimes whether the destruction has gone too far, whether we can really do anything to save our forests and our planet. And yet I know that I can't give up. We must do the right thing because it is the right thing to do regardless of the outcome. I have to take it one struggle at a time. And just as I've done with Luna, when that struggle comes my way, I've got to fight it for all I'm worth.
>
> Yes, one person *can* make a difference. Each one of us does (237–38).

Heroes such as Julia need to be part of every young person's education. Julia Butterfly Hills's story clearly and dramatically reveals the political dimension of education.

Conclusion

Now, we return to my original two questions: What kind of a world do we want to inhabit and, What are schools for? The two clearly are intertwined and schools cannot avoid either by pleading neutrality or objectivity. Because the agents of power are so clearly in control, neutrality is tantamount to tacit compliance. The corporate-culture which now so dominates our society hides behind political subservience, media camouflage, and educational tolerance and obedience. There can be no real democracy when there is no dissent and not even the recognition by educators that anything is wrong. Yet we know much is wrong; inequities, racism, growing disparities of wealth, child poverty, and homelessness are wrong. The corporate-culture is willing to accept these conditions. Schools should not. The next generation of leaders needs to research what is wrong and realize that change is possible.

There is one additional factor we must acknowledge if we embrace the position that a major purpose of education is to transform — and not conform to — the existing order, and if we accept the fact that at least two billion people, or one-third of humanity, can be called oppressed. We need to examine who, therefore, are the oppressors? The answer here is complex. It would be easy to blame corporate CEOs, oligarchies, billionaire employers of the many, though this would be partially true. But *every one* who accepts material blessings in the nations that consume a disproportionate portion of the world's resources and productivity must share the blame. For by accepting unequal shares, we guarantee that others receive tiny shares. The 1.2 billion people who live on less than one dollar a day subsidize the enormous appetites of those of us in the West who consume anywhere from $137 per day (on a $50,000 a year income) to $2,739 per day (on a $1,000,000 a year income).

If this global system of gross inequality and fundamental unfairness is to be changed in any way, then the current and the coming generations of students must be inspired to care! How can this happen if the schools persist in teaching simple-minded mythologies about "our democratic systems" or "our emerging global village?" Schools, if they wish to change the world, must courageously confront the political, social, and economic realities of oppression, exploitation, and inequity. Furthermore, when educators confront the shadow side of their country and its history, students recognize that they are being presented with meaningful issues. They come alive. They become engaged in the process.

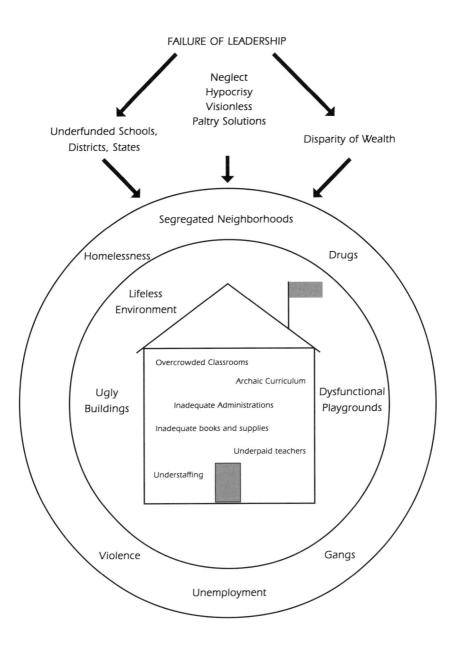

References:

Bellamy, Edward. 1888. *Looking Backward.* (Numerous editions in print).

Croteau, David and William Hoynes. 1994. *By Invitation Only: How the Media Limit Political Debate.* Monroe, ME: Common Courage Press.

Danaher, Kevin, ed. 1996. *Corporations Are Going To Get Your Mama.* Monroe, ME: Common Courage Press.

Freire, Paulo. 1990. *The Pedagogy of the Oppressed.* New York: Continuum.

Galbraith, John Kenneth. 1996. *The Good Society.* New York: Houghton Mifflin Company.

Gutman, Roy and David Rieff, eds. 1999. *Crimes of War.* New York: W.W. Norton & Co.

Hill, Julia Butterfly. 2000. *The Legacy of Luna.* San Francisco: Harper Collins.

Loewen, James W. 1995. *Lies My Teacher Told Me.* New York: The New Press.

Roszak, Theodore. 1973. *Where the Wasteland Ends.* New York: Anchor books.

Vidal, Gore. 1992. *The Decline and Fall of the American Empire.* Berkeley, CA: Odonian Press.

> *That is, you tell a lie by only telling part of the truth. Both sides did it.*
> — William Eastlake
> *The Bamboo Bed*

CHAPTER EIGHT

Nations Confronting Their Shadow

I will never apologize for the
United States. I don't care
what the facts are.
— George Bush Sr.

They are forgetful that the darkness
called night is always present,
Sunlight is the guest.
— Stanley Moss, *The Bathers*

Because God had chosen America as
the construction site of the
earthly paradise, nothing
was ever America's fault.
— Lewis Lapham

All those years we spent jubilant,
Seeing the trifling, cowering world
From the height of our shining saddles,
Brawling our might across the earth
As we forged an empire,
I never questioned . . .
It seemed so clear – our fate was to rule.
That's what I thought at the time.
But perhaps we were merely
Deafened for years by the din
Of our own empire-building,
The shouts of battle, the clanging of words
The cries of victory.
– Aeschylus, *The Persians*

Most students can pretty well apprehend when issues are being presented in a biased manner, glossed over, sentimentalized, or sanitized. For better or worse, they have come to distrust politicians and media spokespersons. In fact, for many thinking students, the whole process of public and civic discourse is suspect. It's hard for them to care for their schoolwork when they sense that they are not being told the truth. Consequently, when teachers pass along various bromides to low income students about the successes of democracy in America, they tune out. Most inner city students see with their own eyes how little regard the government has for their neighborhoods and their plight. "Separation of powers" may be a wonderful topic for a civics discussion, but the separation of power that these students experience has to do with the rich separated from the poor, the CEOs from the workers, the "old boy" power structure from the ghetto dwellings. These separations not only disengage students from their social studies classes and their schools, they also disengage their parents from the election process. The adults don't vote because the system does not work for them, and this atmosphere pervades the neighborhoods where their children grow up.

If teachers want to involve teen students in social studies and contemporary civics classes, they should begin by confronting some of the unpleasant realities of contemporary society. Such classes might, for example, look at the shadow side of history. A psychologist might suggest that in these classes we would "own our shadow."

Dr. Carl Jung provided us with a profound insight about human beings and society, stating that "the ego is what we are and know about consciously; the shadow is that part of us we fail to see or know" (Storr, 212 ff). According to Jung, when we are all born, we have not separated out what is acceptable or unacceptable. Life teaches us these lessons, which vary from society to society. Jungian writer Robert A. Johnson explains: "We are all born whole but somehow the culture demands that we live out only part of our nature and refuse other parts of our inheritance. We divide the self into an ego and a shadow because our culture insists that we behave in a particular manner" (5). In other words, some "bad" characteristics hide within the shadow as well as some "good" characteristics. Consequently, we gain an orderly way to behave in a given society while we lose some levels of diversity, creativity, and ecstasy.

Jung himself saw the shadow in these terms: "By shadow I mean the negative side of the personality, the sum of all those unpleasant qualities we like to hide, together with the insufficiently-developed functions and the contents of the personal unconscious" (Storr, 87). Furthermore, it is not only individuals who are prisoner to the shadow. Nations as well repress their negative characteristics. They do this mostly through the psychic mechanism which Jung referred to as "projecting the shadow."

The shadow is also often projected on others. An examination of those attributes which a man most condemns in other people (greed, intolerance, disregard for others, etc.) usually show that, unacknowledged, he himself possesses them. Jung continues with a passage that is crucial for educators to pass on in the classroom. The passage reveals the essence of this chapter and of a great deal of American history:

Unfortunately there can be no doubt that man is, on the whole, less good than he imagines himself or wants to be. Everyone [and every nation] carries a shadow, and the less it is embodied in the individual's [the nations'] conscious life, the blacker and denser it is . . . if it is repressed and isolated from consciousness, it never gets corrected, and is liable to burst forth suddenly in a moment of unawareness (Storr 88).

The poet Robert Bly puts it this way: "A decision taken privately, as part of one's inner life, to fight the dark side of oneself can cause 'The conscious' and 'The unconscious' to take up adversary positions; and the adversary positions can quickly spread to foreign policy" (14).

There can be no greater challenge for educators in history, social studies, or humanities classes than to occupy students in the examination of the shadow side of America and of other nations. The road from the massacre of the Seminoles (1817) to Wounded Knee (1890) to the suppression of Aguinaldo in the Philippines (1898–1901) to My Lai in Vietnam (1968) is a single road filled with self-justification and attributions of darkness to the victims of our aggression. However, as Jung reminds us, the adversary is none but "the other in me."

In addition to neglecting the shadow, most instructors in schools all across the globe teach what their culture and *its* power structure deems acceptable. Schools are usually very conservative institutions and function to acculturate students into the existing climate. Schools are usually not agents of **re**-form but act more to teach students how to **con**-form. This has the virtue of creating relatively orderly societies, but conversely prevents healthy change and sweeps anything dark under the carpet. Thus we are all taught to disown our national shadow.

To give one example: In American history textbooks, the eighteenth and nineteenth century process of the fledgling United States obtaining its land is often referred to as "the Westward Movement"; that is, colonists moving westward to claim land, to settle, and to build the cities we now know as Dallas, Kansas City, or Los Angeles. What American students usually do not read in those texts is that we claimed this land by stealing it from the people already living there. We murdered Native Americans by the hundreds of thousands and we did all this *in God's name*. We do not teach our children that this was genocide. Nor do American schools teach much about other atrocities committed more recently in Hiroshima, Nagasaki, Dresden, or My Lai. Nor do we talk much about the ongoing racism in our country that began with the aboriginal slavery and continued with every wave of immigration until now. We Americans do not "own" our own shadow very well. In fact, most nations do not do this very well. Our hubris is such that we are even suspicious of history itself. We believe somehow that America is not subject to the lessons and examples which history provides. A recent book review puts it well:

> Americans have cleaved to the conceit that history, insofar as it was deemed important at all, was more hindrance than help in our presumed unstoppable march to the munificent future. Optimistic, pragmatic, impatient, inventive, generous, Americans have refused to be held hostage to history, believing America to have burst its bounds. The cost of such myopia is large. It enfeebles understanding, promotes nostrums of all kinds, and licenses the infantilization of public debate (Wasserman, 3–4).

The failure to acknowledge and, for many, to even recognize our national shadow has enabled America to develop a multi-faceted negative personality. America, of course has its virtues, but that is not the topic at hand. The negatives, of which the Native American massacres and slavery are but two, include such characteristics as overweening "Diplopride," what the Greeks called *Hubris*, arrogance, blindness to the suffering of others, economic rapacity, environmental exploitation, and insensitivity to human rights at home and abroad. Sadly, the failure to recognize and acknowledge past transgressions virtually guarantees their repetition.

Lewis Lapham recently wrote an article "The American Rome" (*Harpers*, August 2001) in which his subtitle, "on the theory of virtuous empire" provides a real insight about American history. We do not recognize the evils we perpetrate because we define ourselves as innately and almost divinely virtuous. It is this self-definition that blinds us to our actions and to how others perceive us. Not only do we claim to be the world's only superpower, but we claim that we have been singled out by God to possess and dispense this power. Whatever we do is, by our definition, "good." For example, examine the blatant expression of arrogance in the United States' relations with Cuba from 1898 to the present day. During this 63-year period, April 21, 1898 to April 21, 1961, the United States acted upon the goal of freeing Cuba from Spanish domination. The U.S. claimed to be enabling Cubans to achieve the same freedoms the United States achieved by throwing off British domination. Instead, the United States, in effect, colonized Cuba to serve United States interests, and when Cubans finally rebelled and sought the freedom the U.S. had promised, then America supported the Batista regime and opposed the rebels. As William Appleton Williams explains in his *The Tragedy of American Diplomacy,* Americans learned little from the history of their own revolution and instead of understanding the desires of Cubans to gain independence, incorrectly blamed communist Russia as controlling Castro: "The stereotype of Soviet influence or control was grossly at odds with the facts" (5). But having made this miscalculation, the U.S.A. pushed Castro into an increasingly close relationship with the Soviet Union.

Then, on April 17, 1961, the U.S. invaded Cuba in the infamous Bay of Pigs fiasco. "The action was a blatant violation of the treaty system that the United States had solemnly created to govern international relations in the Western Hemisphere, and a violation of its own neutrality laws" (Wiliams, 6). The net result was a heightening of "the aura of terror that was developing around American foreign policy." Williams wrote these words in 1972 and since then, that aura of terror has only increased: in Vietnam, Cambodia, and Laos, in Chile, in Grenada and Panama, in Iraq, and the list goes on. Yet, in our eyes, we remain by our own definition good, in spite of the rest of the world which increasingly thinks otherwise. We do not see our shadow.

After the Vietnam War, our focus was upon bringing home the 2,500 or so missing-in-action Americans while ignoring the desperate need to repair the land where we caused between two to three million deaths as well as ecological devastation. As Noam Chomsky writes in *Terrorizing the Neighborhood,* "The trivial fact that the United States had invaded South Vietnam and virtually destroyed it was unthinkable, and remains so" (31). It remains so because goodness cannot be bad. The problem is that this attitude engenders enormous hostility elsewhere and leads us to commit profound acts of cruelty and destruction.

The phenomenon of defining oneself so as to overlook one's own shadow transgressions was supported by an extensive study of high school history texts dealing with the Vietnam War. Chomsky reports in *Rethinking Camelot* that this study found that the word "terror" does not appear *once* in reference to U.S. or client practices in any of the forty-eight texts examined in 1979 and 1990. The Viet Cong, it is duly noted, murdered and terrorized; one can only wonder how they could possibly out-terrorize Diem's U.S. backed forces" (61). Noam Chomsky's response is that "the answer to that question is quite simple: it is true by definition, the same device that expunges the vastly greater U.S. terror, and its aggression itself from the annals of history" (61). This phenomenon is, of course, a clear example of what Jung would call projecting the shadow — attributing the unacceptable and unacknowledged dark forces within oneself to others. In addition, Chomsky writes in *Necessary Illusions: Thought Control in Democratic Societies*: "We have no problem in perceiving the Soviet invasion of Afghanistan as brutal aggression . . . But the U.S. invasion of South Vietnam in the early 1960s . . . cannot be perceived as what it was" (50). After the United States was defeated in Vietnam, American textbooks do not refer to the expulsion of the Americans as a "liberation" for the Vietnamese — now freed from the U.S. opposition to their "democratic struggle for self-determination against foreign aggression" (Marciano,131). Instead, with our characteristic hubris *we* refer to *their* freedom as the "Fall of Vietnam."

America does not like to see itself as an Empire. President Reagan once referred to Russia as an "evil empire" but could not see that this is exactly how many characterize the United States. Thomas E. Weisskopf writes that, "Indeed, a brief review of American history points to a pattern of imperialist behavior that goes back long before the postwar (WW II) period to the beginning of the Federal Republic" (162). Yet, I think Weisskopf's views are not accepted by American politicians, journalists, power brokers, and even the general public. The Native American massacres and African slavery are "the past"; our invasions and colonization of places like the Philippines and Hawaii are simply referred to as annexations; the massive devastation (500,000 of our troops and more bombs than W.W.II) wreaked upon Vietnam, Cambodia, and Laos was simply deterring the spread of communism. Nowhere in any of these examples, and others, is there any sense that America was at fault. Lapham remarks: "Because God had chosen America as the construction site of the earthly paradise, nothing was ever America's fault" (33).

Besides the avoidance of words such as "terror" or "empire" in texts as they might be applied to American action in the world, there is another shadow side to America in the 20th Century which I believe students should confront. In her book, *A Problem From Hell,* Samantha Power dramatically shines the light into this shadowy terrain: It is the history of those individuals who have stood up to unfolding genocides in the world as their countries have stood passively and indifferently on the sidelines. Her book focuses upon American inactivity while international tragedies evolved that the U.S. might have prevented. Students will find this topic compelling and engaging. "Never again" is a meaningful phrase only when the next generation is educated to understand the horrible consequences of denial and inaction.

I have been astonished over the past fifteen years in discussions with foreign students to discover how little they know of twentieth century atrocities committed in their own countries. Russian students know little of Stalin's treatment of Russian peasants during the 1930s and the murderous purges of 1936–38, "The Great Terror." Taiwanese students know little of Chang Kai-Shek's assassinations and mass murdering of local Taiwanese tribes when he took over the island. Mainland Chinese students know virtually nothing of Mao's progressive irrationalities, of the millions who died during the 1950s "Great Leap Forward," and of the brutalities of the 1960s Cultural Revolution. So it goes across the globe.

If each nation in the world were to acknowledge its shadow side, a great deal of current animosity between many nations might be alleviated and future conflicts might be prevented. Looking objectively at the shadow can serve as a form of restraint: when we become aware of own transgressions, perhaps we will not be so quick to attack others for their perceived transgressions.

It would be a stunning achievement for American, and for *all* nations' educators to confront the issues outlined in this chapter and to engage students in the process. Every culture has its dichotomies and contradictions. Most are unwilling to deal with them. And so on it goes, generation after generation, perpetuating the habits and shortcomings of the previous generations. We call this "tradition," but sometimes that label "tradition" is at best unreflective inertia and at worst repressed darkness. Nevertheless, some fellow educators and I keep hoping, writing, teaching, with the thought that progress, though elusive, is still a possibility. The American poet Emily Dickinson, wrote "I dwell in possibility." It is a good place in which to dwell.

References:

Bly, Robert. 1988. *A Little Book on the Human Shadow.* San Francisco, Harper Collins.

Chomsky, Noam. 1991. *Terrorizing the Neighborhood.* San Francisco: Pressure Drop Press.

———. 1993. *Rethinking Camelot.* Boston: South End Press.

———. 1989. *Necessary Illusions: Thought Control In Democratic Societies.* Boston: South End Press.

Johnson, Robert A. 1991. *Owning Your Own Shadow.* San Francisco: Harper Collins.

Lapham, Lewis. August 2001, "The American Rome: On the Theory of Virtuous Empire," Harpers Magazine.

Marciano, John. 1977. *Civic Illiteracy and Education.* New York: Peter Lang.

Power, Samantha. 2002. *"A Problem From Hell": America and the Age of Genocide.* New York: Basic Books.

Storr, Anthony, ed. 1983. *The Essential Jung.* Princeton: The Princeton University Press.

Wasserman, Steve. Sept. 23, 2001. "Future Shock" (Review). Los Angeles Times, 3–4.

Weisskopf, Thomas E. as quoted in Ikenberry, John G. 1989. *American Foreign Policy.* (p.162.) New York: Harper Collins.

Williams, William Appleton. 1988. *The Tragedy of American Diplomacy.* New York: Norton.

> *Only conceit, dreams of grandeur, vain imaginings, lust for power, or a desire to escape from our domestic perils and obligations could possibly make us suppose that providence has appointed us his chosen people for the pacification of the earth.*
>
> —Charles Beard (1939)

V

OPPOSITES: TESTING AND THE ARTS

The thing was to get now and then elated.
— Robert Frost

CHAPTER NINE

Testing: Great is Our Sin

If the misery of our poor be caused,
not by the laws of nature, but by
our institutions, great is our sin.
— Charles Darwin
Voyage of the Beagle

One sees clearly only with the heart.
Anything essential is invisible to the eyes.
— Antoine de Saint Exupéry
The Little Prince

It is as cruel to bore a child
as to beat him or her.
— George B. Leonard
Education and Ecstasy

In this era of accountability and holding students to higher standards for promotion, testing is certainly a fact of life. Certainly, we must do more than just rail against tests without offering any alternatives or ways of keeping testing balanced and in proportion to other higher educational values. Nevertheless, if we are to provide students with a valuable education, then we must re-examine the value of tests. What do they really measure and what is the significance of these measurements? Students will devalue the process of learning if we continue to stress the importance of what they clearly see as patently unimportant. In fact, the only lesson they will really learn from our obsessive reliance on standardized testing is that "education" (i.e., preparing for tests) is a means to other ends and is *not* an end in itself. Grades and test scores are the equivalent of cash for young people. They are education's version of materialism, and material pursuits are essentially hollow. Many students know this. Educators today need to find the courage to resist the seemingly easy solutions — such as testing purports to be — and to find alternative ways of defining and measuring what is truly important.

Recently, while re-reading Stephen Jay Gould's excellent book, *The Mismeasure of Man*, I came across the above quote of Charles Darwin.

Great indeed is our sin. Our sin in this case consists of imposing on our young a deadening new version of an old and stultifying view of what is important in education. Our sin is imposing a common denominator through a common set of curricular goals upon all young people in a given subject and then reducing that to a common evaluation of diverse youngsters. Our current, early 21st century testing mania stresses "standards," but often utilizes teaching styles and subject matter that are trivial and boring.

Do I believe in standards? I certainly do believe in teaching students how to write in clear and coherent prose, in offering progressively more complex mathematical calculations, and in performing scientific investigations. These standards, however, evolve from dense and demanding curricula; they can not be reduced to a multiple choice, machine-scored test. Yet, across the land, politicians, school boards, and even educators pound the table demanding tougher standards, accountability, and state and national tests to measure our progress. All this table thumping makes the thumper appear tough-minded and "good-old-fashioned," as if proclaiming something significant. Anyone who tries to question the underlying assumptions is quickly dismissed as a wimp, a progressive, or even a "rock-the-boat" liberal. Americans, particularly politicians and pundits, have never dealt well with complexity or ambiguity. We crave simple statements with simple answers. The current mess in education, unfortunately, does not lend itself to simple answers. I wish to get beyond table thumping, summarize current thinking, and propose some new directions regarding the testing obsession overshadowing the educational landscape.

In 1999, Nicholas Lemann wrote an important book, *The Big Test: The Secret History of the American Meritocracy*. The book provided a valuable service in offering a history of the notorious SAT. Once designated the Scholastic Aptitude Test, it is now simply the SAT because the name was misleading and perhaps even cruel. Lemann's history reveals ironies, as well as some disturbing and uncomfortable cultural realities which we do not like to acknowledge. One irony is that the SAT — which really came into prominence after World War II — was designed to allow for an intellectual meritocracy rather than one of privilege. James Bryant Conant, the President of Harvard during the 1930s and 1940s, envisioned the SAT as creating a democratic opportunity for poorer students to enter a Harvard or Yale by doing well on the test that supposedly measured aptitude. Thus, not just children of wealthy alumni would be admitted to prestigious colleges, but students selected for merit alone could be admitted regardless of their background. Unfortunately, the SAT has failed in this purpose and is today just another tool for the privileged students to solidify and perpetuate that privilege.

The racial bias of the SATs and of standardized testing in general may be entirely unintended. For now, let us make that assumption. Whatever the intentions are, however, it is the results that matter. The fact is that college admissions officers seriously weigh SAT verbal and math scores as significant criteria for college acceptance. The very fact that ETS dropped the word "aptitude" out of the SAT definition would affirm that the test measures something other than aptitude. In fact it contains a heavy measure of something else: privilege. A child born into a low-income family with no history of higher education, attending an under-funded school, a school where a high percentage of teachers are not qualified to teach their subjects, and living in a violent, drug-infested, run-down neighborhood will generally ***not*** do as well on a standardized test as will a child growing up in a comfortably middle-class home and neighborhood. As the title of Carl Upchurch's autobiography reveals, the poor, inner-city child has been "condemned in the womb."

The SAT not only rewards those being born in nicer neighborhoods and attending better schools, but now those who can take added advantage of the tutor-test coaching business. This new half-billion dollar industry, available almost exclusively to the privileged, attracts students who can essentially purchase higher scores. This service comes at a high price, from $150 to $350 an hour for private tutors, or up to $415 for private sessions with organizations such as Advantage Testing. Many students attend weekly sessions, often twice a week. Over the course of an academic year, the cost can be as high as $25,000 — nearly the average annual cost of tuition, room and board at one of the prestigious colleges that most of these students hope to attend. These typically private school students receive their instruction at Advantage, or Kaplan, or Princeton Review, and then take the SATs along with poor and minority students who take the test cold. Is it any surprise who does better? According to Christopher Jencks and Meredith Phillips, authors of *The Black-White Test Score Gap*, "lower test scores by blacks are the single biggest barrier to racial equality in this country." As Tony Schwartz writes in the New York Times, "Whatever effects coaching has on SAT results, it's clear that those who need it most are often getting it least. Hundreds of thousands of youngsters from economically disadvantaged backgrounds don't have the same access to test preparation that kids from more affluent families take for granted" (p. 51). Clearly, the process is unfair.

Lemann begins *The Big Test* with a look at the advent of the intelligence quotient test. First used in the 1900s to assign army jobs during World War I, the IQ was also used by others to support various racist agendas. One of these was the author of the first SAT, Carl Brightman, whose 1922 book *A Study of Intelligence* was an anti European-immigration polemic. Later, however, Brightman retracted his racist interpretation of the IQ and issued the following rather extraordinary statement:

> The test movement came to this country some twenty-five or thirty years ago accompanied by one of the most glorious fallacies in the history of science, namely, that the tests measured "native intelligence" purely and simply without training or schooling. I hope nobody believes that now. The test scores very definitely are a composite including schooling, family background, familiarity with English, and everything else. The native intelligence hypothesis is dead (quoted in Phillips-Fein, 114).

The first president of Educational Testing Services (ETS), Henry Chauncey, also saw the SAT as a means of "fulfilling Alexander Hamilton's promise to reduce the idea of 'accident and force' in life especially in the creation of social class" (Phillips-Fein, 114). So, from Brightman and Chauncey to Conant to Clark Kerr at the University of California, the SAT was originally seen as the great equalizer. However, it certainly has been nothing of the sort. Ultimately, the SAT has become a dominant factor in college admissions offices, but it has not served the underserved very well. In addition to being a superficial test, it has become a tool of well-to-do children and has not advanced the cause of meritocracy. As Kim Phillips-Fein points out, the primary factor in college admissions is class or caste. When one-half to three-quarters of all personal wealth in the United States can be traced to inheritance, we can see that education and an SAT test aren't going to change much. "Fifty years after Conant, the children of Harvard alumni are still twice as likely to get into their parents' alma mater as everyone else" (115). Or, as another writer reminds us, "The strongest correlation that exists to future success is family income" (Schwartz, 30). As we will see, the SAT coaching industry predominantly available to the wealthier in society renders the SAT, and more recently AP tests, as "just another privilege of privilege" (Schwartz, 31).

If this is so, if the SAT does not help to level the playing field, what kind of a test is it? What does it do? What value does it really offer us educationally and culturally?

Well, as to what kind of a test it is, quite simply it is a three-hour standardized test. It is what we call a high-stakes test (your college future may be at risk); it is *not* an aptitude or even a comprehensive curricular test; it is a multiple-choice, machine-scored test, which reduces the student's performance to a single score (a verbal score and a mathematics score); it does *not* cover science or history or any of the arts; and, finally, as one coaching company head says, "the SAT measures a limited, fairly primitive range of mental abilities and those not very well" (Schwartz, 32).

The test rationale, according to Julian Weissglass, is based on several faulty assumptions:

♦ One, that it is possible to measure understanding and potential with reasonable accuracy and communicate it meaningfully;

♦ Two, that standardized testing does not interfere with student learning;

♦ three, that it is possible to design standardized tests that are *not* culturally, gender or class biased;

♦ And four, that student performance on the test is independent of the testing environment and culture of the school.

None of these assumptions are true. Weissglass goes on to provide five telling arguments:

- ♦ One, no person's understanding or potential can be reduced to a number and it is disrespectful to do so;

- ♦ Two, standardized testing interferes with student learning by increasing anxiety and coercing students to memorize for the test rather than focus on learning;

- ♦ Three, testing leads teachers to focus on test scores rather than students as complex learners;

- ♦ Four, it is beyond our current capacity to design bias-free standardized tests;

- ♦ Five, performance on tests depends on the classroom environment, the cultural climate of the school, as well as the societal messages internalized by standards regarding their intelligence.

Daniel Greenberg, in examining the Massachusetts Comprehensive Assessment System, provides his own list of faulty assumptions relevant to the SATs, as well as just about any standardized high-stakes test:

- ♦ One, that all children undergo the same developmental process, at the same basic rate from birth until maturity;

- ♦ Two, that the same extensive body of knowledge must be possessed by every single person in order for society to function successfully [a patently untrue notion in an age of massive information as well as specialization];

- ♦ Three, that material covered on the tests is important knowledge [Greenberg calls it trivial and preoccupied with naming things rather than understanding them];

- ♦ Four, that the tests measure something significant about a person's ability to perform a given task with proficiency.

Pausing and reflecting, we see that the tests are often biased, trivial, not connected to school curricula, limited in scope in that they ignore most subjects, and are developmentally inappropriate. Yet they have not only taken root, but are being pushed as the salvation of a faltering education system. The importance of the SAT and APs in securing college acceptances is so enormous that it has spawned a new industry of test preparation. As we have seen even the founder of the Princeton Review Company speaks of the SATs with utter disdain, stating that they are "pernicious, meaningless bullsh-t, foisted upon America's youth by a greedy corporation" (Katzman).

Perhaps the most outspoken critic of high-stakes testing is Alfie Kohn. Kohn's most recent book, *The Case Against Standardized Testing: Raising the Scores, Ruining the Schools*, is a virtual jeremiad, one that every school teacher and principal should read. Kohn cites eight facts about standardized testing, some of which I have already mentioned (in discussing Weissglass and Greenberg), but Kohn's eight arguments are worthy of listing here.

1. Our children are tested to an extent that is unprecedented and unparalleled anywhere else in the world;

2. Non-instructional factors explain most of the variance among test scores when schools or districts are compared;

3. Non-reference tests were never intended to measure the quality of learning or teaching;

4. Standardized test scores often measure superficial thinking;

5. Virtually all specialists condemn the practice of giving standardized tests to children younger than 8 or 9 years old;

6. Virtually all relevant experts and organizations condemn the practice of basing important decisions, such as graduation or promotion, on the results of a single test;

7. The time, energy, and money that are being devoted to preparing students for standardized tests must come from somewhere;

8. Many educators are leaving the field because of what is being done to schools in the name of accountability and tougher standards.

When you add up the objections to standardized testing, SATs and high-stakes testing, the arguments appear so overwhelming and persuasive that few could disagree. Yet standardized testing (for which "standards" is often a code word) is on the rise and threatens to overwhelm our public schools. Like a snowball gathering momentum, standardized testing is rolling down the hill faster and faster, smothering voices of reason and caution with political and societal platitudes. Vacuous statements such as: "I believe in standards" create the illusion of having said something of importance when in reality they are unsubstantial and may even contribute to our educational morass. What they do to students is to reinforce their feelings of education's shallowness.

We have thus far seen the educational objections to standardized testing and to SATs as presented by Weissglass, Greenberg, and Kohn. There are dozens of others (see the bibliography to this chapter) most of which reiterate the arguments listed above, though a few more are worth mentioning:

Linda Nathan: It is a faulty notion that "if we test more, schools will improve" (*Harvard Education Letter*, May/June 2000).

Nicholas Lemann: SATs don't measure demonstrated achievement in a given field; they measure quick reading and quick problem solving — "a mindless ability to take trivial tests" (NY Review, 22).

Alan Ryan: the Princeton Review Company has "flourished by working out that what the SAT really measures is the ability to read the minds of the people who set the test" (Ryan, NY Review, 23).

Barbara Miner: A confusion of standards with standardized testing "leads to a dumbed down curriculum that values rote memorization over in-depth thinking, exacerbates inequities for low-income students and students of color, and undermines true accountability among schools, parents and community" (41).

To the various objections listed above, I would like to add one of my own. When the accountability-testing, standardized-machine-scored, multiple-choice, single-answer, single-score tests-mind set takes over, it kills the spirit of schools. Standardized testing leads to joyless classrooms and schools. Decontextualized memorization and attention to learning lists of things bores teachers and students alike, banishing creative thinking. Standardized test questions each have a single answer to them, one designed by someone else. Students must figure out what single answer someone else wants. No room remains for individual questioning, and any attempt at an imaginative response to the question is fatal. Convergent thinking is the essence of standardized testing; divergent thinking leads to disaster. Yet it is divergent thinkers that the world needs. Businesses worldwide bemoan the lack of problem solvers. In our world of rapidly changing technology, people trained to spew out yesterday's facts are useless. Nevertheless, this is what we seem determined to produce.

Finally, there is one additional faulty assumption: that a single-score, single-answer test measures anything valuable. In fact, I would counter with e.e. cummings' assertion that "it is my firm conviction that nothing measurable is worth a good god damn." The things that are essential in education and in life are not reducible to tests. The more time we require teachers to teach to a test, prepare students for the test, take practice tests, and then actually take the tests, semester after semester, year after year, the more we crush the spirit of students and depress the whole educational scene. As the fox tells the Little Prince in Saint Exupéry's classic, "one sees clearly only with the heart. Anything essential is invisible to the eyes." Yet we threaten to drive a stake into the heart of education with our obsession for testing.

So what is to be done about all this, given the degree to which the testing mania and testing industry dominate the current scene? Well, for one, high school and colleges alike must find the courage to implement alternative means of measuring student achievement. Second, public school teachers and administrators need to lobby against the curricular take-over by standardized testing. Third, teachers need to find ways to teach test-taking skills as one separate skill within a whole body of skills to be learned, and to avoid having the test-taking skill dominate curriculum content.

Schools should be places of adventure and meaning, places that children look forward to attending each day, places where exploration and inventiveness are the guiding lights. Yes, students must learn skills. They must learn to read well, write accurately and stylistically, to calculate and think clearly. However, none of this should be at the expense of the joy of learning. We need not hand over our educational vision to what H.L. Mencken referred to as the "American Booboisie," to the George F. Babbitts of the nation. We need to listen to our best educational minds, the Howard Gardners and Jonathan Kozols, and Alfie Kohns. If our institutions force meaning and joy out of our children's education, it would indeed be a great sin.

References:

Greenberg, Daniel. Autumn 1999. "The Case Against Standardized Tests." *Paths of Learning,* 32–38.

Kohn, Alfie. 2000. *The Case Against Standardized Testing.* Portsmouth, New Hampshire: Heinemann.

Lemann, Nicholas. Quoted in review of Alan Ryan (see below).

Miner, Barbara. August 2000. "Making the Grade," *The Progressive.*

Nathan, Linda. May/June, 2000. *Harvard Education Letter.*

Phillips-Fein, Jim. Spring 2000. "The Meritocracy Trap," *Dissent,* 113–116.

Ryan, Alan. Nov. 18, 1999. "The Twisted Path to the Top," *New York Review of Books.*

Schwartz, Tony. Jan. 10, 1999. "The Test Under Stress," *The New York Times Magazine.*

Weissglass, Julian. April 15, 1998. "The SAT: Public-Spirited or Pre-serving Privilege?" *Education Week,* 60, 45.

> *It is of no avail to speak
> of the ocean to a frog in a well.*
> — Old Chinese Proverb

CHAPTER TEN

The Arts: Transformation, Discovery, Surprise

God guard me from those thoughts men think
In the mind alone,
He that sings a lasting song
Thinks in a marrow bone.
— W.B. Yeats

Will you, won't you, will you, won't you, will you join the dance?
Will you, won't you, will you, won't you, won't you join the dance?
— Lewis Carroll

There is no more rapid, immediate, and dynamic way of engaging students than through the arts. Creating a piece of sculpture, improvising even the most rudimentary sounds on a drum, acting out a scene one has written alone or in collaboration, all provide immediate feedback. A student struggling with a landscape drawing will eagerly receive practical instruction on achieving perspective or creating a shadow effect. The thrill of immediacy is enhanced by any number of applied skills taught in the classroom or studio. The arts are capable of capturing the student's mind and imagination in ways no other subject can, and cannot be relegated to *extra*-curricular or after-school status. In my previous book on education, *For Mortal Stakes,* I made a case for the importance of the arts by offering twelve arguments. Before making several additional arguments I will repeat them here, briefly:

1. The arts help us communicate about transcendent values and issues;

2. The arts offer non-academic achievers another avenue to success;

3. The arts provide a common language in a complex global culture;

4. They help develop innovative thinkers;

5. They help reduce negative self-expression;

6. They help provide jobs, audiences, tourism;

7. They improve graduation rates;

8. They teach cooperation and creative problem solving;

9. They help develop leadership-artists push the boundaries;

10. They inspire self-confidence;

11. They energize and beautify school campuses;

12. They help students learn how to honor the Earth.

Each of these requires full explanation, but perhaps just listing them here will stimulate some speculation about their significance. I want to present several other arguments in favor of expanding the arts in our schools. It is discouraging that the arts need advocates and activistic proponents and that their value is not self-evident to all. Ours may be the first society to struggle with the role of art. Therefore, let's look at how the arts engage students and why art's special blend of magic is so crucial for the students' development and for society's health.

Students in many schools across the nation walk or bus to school through utterly depressing streets and neighborhoods. They may not articulate their daily travels as such, but there is nothing beautiful or uplifting about what they see. They live in settings which brutalize the human spirit. Most inner cities are simply ugly. Those who have money flee and raise their children in tree-lined streets with well tended lawns and verdant and colorful flower gardens. They may send their children to private schools, which are also attractive and well-maintained. But a large number of American children today attend ugly schools in ugly neighborhoods. And what does this do to the human spirit but depress it?

The arts, however, are a combative force. They teach students to transform the ugliness around them into beauty; children take ordinary materials and make something new, interesting and delightful. Even dark themes bring pleasure in the making; it is all, in some strange way, swept up in the delight of the picture. Even the gloomiest of paintings may bring satisfaction and delight in the art of image-making. I have watched teachers help students to make profound social commentary by forging plastics, consumer waste materials and broken objects into startling montages. Murals on gray, drab colored buildings, student art work lining bare school halls, even controlled graffiti on cement walls can transform the banal into exciting new creations. The message to students is clear: No matter what difficulties life has placed upon you, you need not accept it as such; you can rebel and transform your emotions into something to uplift the human spirit.

This process of transformation belongs to another deep virtue of the arts: the process of self-discovery. Whatever art form a student stumbles upon, or is introduced to by a teacher or artist, the result is often that of discovery. I *can* do this; I do enjoy that; I have a talent for this; I have something to say that I never knew before. As musician and artist Herb Alpert writes: "Through my art I am continuously trying to explain myself to myself." When a teacher provides even a modicum of support or encouragement, the results are often dramatic. There are two extraordinary examples of this process to relate. Both happened to young men languishing in maximum security prisons.

In a Los Angeles courtroom in 1955, a street punk named Rick Cluthey, a recent arrival from Detroit, was sentenced to life imprisonment without possibility of parole for kidnapping, robbing, and shooting a middle-aged executive. He was sent to San Quentin where his ability to fight earned him respect and freedom from various kinds of assaults.

On November 19, 1957, his life changed. The warden of San Quentin allowed a performance in the prison by the San Francisco Actor's Workshop of Samuel Beckett's *Waiting for Godot*. Cluthey was astounded. The play, he recalls, made sense to the inmates who spent every day of their lives waiting for some appearance of salvation.

Cluthey and several other inmates, inspired by the play, requested permission to form a theatre group. A performer from the *Godot* production, Alan Mandell, came to the prison to teach acting classes and recognized Cluthey's talent. For more than six years, Mandell made weekly visits to San Quentin teaching directing, acting, and writing.

In 1965, Cluthey wrote a prison drama, *The Cage*, which conveyed "The disintegration of the human animal behind walls." Mandell, meanwhile, had led an effort to get Cluthey out of jail and, in 1964, on his last day of office before he surrendered the Governorship to recently elected Ronald Reagan, Pat Brown allowed the parole board the option to consider life parole.

Finally, on a foggy day in December 1966, Rick Cluthey — after eleven years, nine months and fourteen days in prison — was released from San Quentin. He worked in several theatre groups and, in 1974, was invited to perform in *Waiting for Godot* in Berlin, with Nobel Prize winner Samuel Beckett directing! A strong bond developed between the two, and later Alan Mandell joined Cluthey in performances of Beckett plays. The circle had closed and Rick Cluthey's life, by now somewhat of a fairy tale, underwent a complete transformation. What had changed his life was witnessing the performance of a play in prison.

As the title of his book poignantly declares, Carl Upchurch was *Convicted in the Womb*. Born in South Philadelphia (1950) to a stern, cold, disapproving mother and an absentee father, (murdered at the age of 32, when Carl was twelve), Carl became a street punk, an elementary school drop-out (after being humiliated in third grade by his teacher), and a gang member and criminal. His crimes grew progressively worse and he was, he believes, brutalized by the environment in which he grew up:

> In South Philly, violence was so commonplace that I grew up believing it was the solution to every problem. I emulated the people I saw — hoodlums, gangsters, and slick criminals. My heroes were those who were quick with a fist, a knife, or a gun.

Carl progressed from petty theft and fighting to grand larceny and aggravated assault, and from juvenile detention to hard time. Once in prison, he got into one fight after another and spent long periods in solitary confinement. He describes what happened during one of these confinements:

> The only emotion I knew how to express was rage. I spent days in solitary at Lewisburg, lying on my bunk, silently raging at what I was convinced was an unjust legal system. By pure accident there was a book in my cell. One leg of the gray table was shorter than the other three, and someone had

stuck a thin book beneath it. I pulled it out and stared at the cover in disgust. It was Shakespeare's Sonnets. I won't pretend that Shakespeare and I immediately connected. I must have read those damn sonnets twenty times before they started to make sense. Even then comprehension came slowly — first a word, then a phrase, then a whole poem. Those sonnets transported me out of the gray world into a world I had never, ever imagined. That book of sonnets didn't just change my opinion; it quite literally changed my mind. I discovered the magic of learning, the thrill of going from not knowing to knowing. By struggling to understand Shakespeare, I came to see that ideas have a beauty all their own, beyond even the beauty of the words that frame them (81–83).

Carl Upchurch is now the founder and executive director of the Council for Urban Peace and Justice in Pittsburgh, PA. He lectures widely on the state of urban affairs and has addressed audiences at major universities and conferences as well as the United Nations. The accident of a thin book of sonnets left in his prison cell changed his life. Such is the magic of the arts.

The question that lurks behind this story is: How many young Ricks or Carls across the country grow up in brutal surroundings from which they never emerge? How many children are denied the opportunity to develop their intelligence, their talents, and ultimately, their humanity because of ghetto deprivation? How many children are deprived of arts classes that might enable them to find self-expression through self-discovery and self-confidence? Carl Upchurch's extraordinary story is just that, *extra* ordinary. He stumbled upon Shakespeare as Rick Cluthey stumbled upon Beckett. These are but two stories of the many, often untold stories that validate the place of the arts: at the *center* of the curriculum.

In the cases of Carl Upchurch and Rick Cluthey, while the arts physically released them from a societal prison, a form of art also released them from a prison of lonely, mean, and meaningless lives. Their inner walls were as crippling as those of their pre-prison and in-prison buildings. Yet, look what it took: for Rick, a play and a drama teacher; for Carl, a discarded copy of Shakespeare's sonnets. Some hundreds of thousands of dollars of incarceration costs for these two men were redeemed by chance exposures to the arts. They were removed from being "in disgrace with fortune and men's eyes" by being *allowed* to create and discover who they were in life-affirming ways.

Or consider yet another story. R., a Latina student, graduated from our New Roads High school in Santa Monica, California in 2001. Through the arts, she learned to not reject life, but to celebrate and embrace it. R. came to the attention of two of our music teachers in the fourth grade. She liked the plastic recorder provided to her and her classmates. She developed some skills in playing it and was selected for an advanced ensemble. She was given a more expensive, real wood instrument and her sight reading and playing skills continued to improve. Nevertheless, R. lived in a depressing neighborhood under extraordinarily hard conditions at home. She moved on to a nearby public middle school and it was a struggle to keep her focused on her music. Gangs, drugs, and peer pressure all militated against her participating in a small woodwind ensemble. Several times we thought we had lost her to the undercurrents of the Barrio.

Yet, somehow her music kept a hold on her. We accepted her into New Roads in the 8th grade, gave her an orchestral instrument and provided her with private lessons. Her music became the lifeline to a better world. The discipline required to play recorder and flute was applied to her academics and her grades began to improve. Attending a school where everyone talked about not just going to college, but *which* college, rubbed off on her. The name Ann Arbor, which had captured her imagination as a child, was the name she latched onto when college discussions took place at school. In the fall of 2001, as the first college attendee ever from her family, R. began her studies on a full scholarship at the University of Michigan at Ann Arbor, and is studying English and American Literature.

R's story, as well as the story of Rick Cluthey and Carl Upchurch, illustrates another virtue of the arts and demonstrates further why the arts must be accorded permanent and prominent place in our school's curricula. We live in a culture where, as Morris Berman writes, consumerism reigns supreme:

> If the twentieth century was the American century, the twenty-first will be the Americanized century, and it will have its roots in a new global economy, in which consumerism will be a full-blown religion (167).

The arts are a critical antidote to this phenomenon which I regard not just as a religion, but as a toxic religion. Consumerism is a cancer which eats away at the soul and renders its victims spiritually razed. People who worship at the altar of materialism cannot escape a sense of meaninglessness. Things do not offer relationships; they only breed an insatiable desire for *more*, thus compounding the feelings of meaninglessness. The act of creation, however, is a powerful corrective. When we consume, in effect, we *ingest* — we acquire someone else's artifact; however, when we create, we do not ingest, we *express*. Students know the difference. Their eyes come alive when they show you a self-portrait or mask they have just made. In the malls their eyes go dull. Our schools need to maximize opportunities for the students to express something of their inner world, for it is here where many begin to see that there is a deeper meaning to education and to life.

In the act of creation, students not only gain the aforementioned virtues, they begin to forge a relationship with the very art materials themselves. They don't just use materials; they perceive them as means of attuning themselves to the world. For example, color becomes not just a statement of fashion or advertising, but an expression from deep inside oneself. In his startling book, *The Spell of the Sensuous*, David Abrams articulates the possibilities of this relationship:

> Genuine art, we might say, is simply human creation that does not stifle the nonhuman element but, rather, allows whatever is Other in the materials to continue to live and to breathe. Genuine artistry, in this sense, does not impose a wholly external form upon some ostensibly "inert" matter, but rather allows the form to emerge from the participation and reciprocity between the artist and his materials, whether these materials be stones, or pigments, or spoken words. Thus understood, art is really a cooperative endeavor, a world of co-creation in which the dynamism and power of earth-born materials is honored and respected. In return for this respect, these materials contribute their more-than-human resonances to human culture (278).

In this process of working with their materials, students also develop a sense of self-discipline. Art requires learning to care passionately about tiny details, as well as formulating a design. Of course, once the concept of self-discipline and the internalization of the concept occurs in one arena, it may be applied in other arenas. A few years ago, we created an after-school arts program at a boys/girls club. One boy was particularly difficult. He was about eleven, defiant, unmotivated in school. He could not read, and he was highly disruptive. We put him in a percussion class. At first, he just banged away at the drums, but the instructor gradually began to teach him patterns. He improved. One day, his school teacher called the boys/girls club and said, "What's going on there? Ricky is starting to read!" What was going on was that Ricky had become fascinated by the process of organizing sounds and the notation representing them. The fascination came in music; the skills were then transferred to reading.

As the culture becomes more and more consumed with consuming, students, in fact all of us, also lose the ability to think clearly. In his recent study, *In the Age of Distraction*, Joseph R. Urgo argues that:

> In such a milieu, the cognitive processes associated with a liberal education — the ability to sort the trivial from the significant, the habits of interrogation and interpretation — are not simply elite luxuries but mechanisms of general survival (94).

Urgo states further that "The threats that face the educationally unprepared in the United States today are gullibility, boredom, listlessness, and vulnerability to intellectual predators" (95). Again, the arts are a forceful antidote. Students learn to sort the trivial from the significant; they learn how to make choices that matter; and they learn life-time pursuits to ward off boredom and listlessness.

Boredom and listlessness, which are certainly sad by-products of the consumerist, shopping-mall, entertainment-saturated practices into which our young are inculcated, result from the very predictability of these practices. Unfortunately, schools themselves are part of this very predictability. Large classes, the teacher at the front talking and talking, homework, dull quizzes and tests, bigger tests and standardized tests, and high stakes tests. Day after day, week after week, year after year. No wonder so few students are excited by the process. No wonder so many drop out. But there is one arena in which the missing ingredient, surprise, can transpire. The arts, when taught even moderately well, provide that element of surprise. When presented with a blank canvas and water colors, students often astonish themselves, particularly if they are not over-programmed. D.H. Lawrence describes the experience: "It is to me the most exciting moment when you have a blank canvas and a big brush full of wet color, and you plunge" (Ghiselin, 69).

It is in such moments where revelation occurs, where the transformation process can happen and where life is celebrated and embraced. Those moments often occur when we combine the blank canvas with another missing ingredient in the students' lives: silence. Blank canvases are rare, for the producers of modern goods pre-package everything. Similarly, silence is antithetical to commercialism, but often a necessary precursor to creativity. In silence, we can hear our inner voices. In silence, we can listen to natural sounds, even silence itself. The concentrated silence of an art studio, a pre-teaching period of quiet in a music class or a theater will facilitate the moments of surprise.

The blank canvas, the absence of noise, whatever way we can provide it for students, facilitates not only inward listening, but witnessing. In her essay, "Teaching A Stone to Talk," Annie Dillard writes that "We are here to witness." Though everyone dies, the beautiful diversity of the world is ours to witness and celebrate: to write about, to paint, to enact on stage, to choreograph, to compose; in sum, to praise. If we fail to communicate this to our students, we fail them on the most profound level. Clearly, the arts are not peripheral to learning; they are at the eye of the storm.

Not only are the arts central to lifelong learning, they have been identified by educational scholar Howard Gardner as encompassing three of "the seven kinds of intelligence" he has categorized. These three are: musical, kinesthetic, and visual-spatial. High quality schools allow for students to express their innate talents and intelligences in all seven of Gardner's categories (the other four are: linguistic, mathematical, inter-personal, and intra-personal). A good school, I believe, is measured by its provision of a wide variety of offerings in music, dance, theatre, and the visual arts.

Also, I believe we can widen Gardner's categories a little farther. Each art form contains different varieties of intelligences, or perhaps we need to add words such as inclinations or predilections, talents, innate understandings. Certain students, for whatever reason, gravitate not only to a given art form, but to areas of expression within that art form. Thus, in music one of the abilities is tonal recognition, the ability to discriminate between subtle sound differences. Some musicians have perfect pitch. For example, my wife will hear me playing a piano piece and, if I hit a wrong note, will shout from another room: "B Flat!" or whatever. Her ear immediately hears the correct tone. This is a kind of intelligence that is uncommon but which needs to be encouraged just as much as gifted intelligence in mathematics or linguistic areas.

In music there are other "intelligences" such as rhythmic — the ability to hear and reproduce complicated patterns; melodic — the ability to hear and create phrases and ideas in sound; harmonic — the ability to see the inter-relationship of chords and successions of tone clusters; composition — the ability to create entire pieces; performance — voice and instrumental skills. Some specific talents of visual arts are: 1) to arrange colors and materials into pleasing shapes and patterns; 2) to express a private vision of the world; 3) to create harmony and unity from disparate images. In dance: 1) the ability to perform; 2) to internalize emotions and express them in body movement; 3) to choreograph and create new patterns and styles. And in theatre it is: 1) the ability to create characters on stage; 2) to create stage scenes; 3) to choreograph scenes; 4) to direct; 5) to write scripts.

In a school which truly honors the arts, each of the above intelligences-skills-talents-inclinations would be encouraged. Furthermore, when their students are activated, the entire school becomes enlivened. Nothing so transforms any given campus as dramatically as a dynamic arts program.

There are three other reasons for placing the arts at the center of the curriculum: 1) to cultivate our students' respect for beauty; 2) to inspire them to protect the world's treasures of natural wonders and its creatures; and 3) to affirm the value of individuality. The first cannot occur without concurrently developing in students an awareness of ugliness. To respect beauty often necessitates an understanding of its opposite. Taste is, admittedly, a subjective matter; however, it must be considered in the classroom. We have large numbers of students graduating from high school who have never taken any courses in the arts and have a meager sense of aesthetics. In addition, large numbers of drop outs have grown up in ugly industrial wastelands and have never seen anything beautiful — neither natural landscapes nor artistic renditions, neither architectural monuments nor pictures of great architecture. They have read little, if any, works by masterful writers, and are bombarded with insipid commercial language. They are desensitized by their environment and their potential for responsiveness to anything beautiful is under-nourished at school. As C.S. Lewis writes, "We castrate and bid the geldings be fruitful" (*Abolition*, 35).

The second reason, as articulated by Wendell Berry in *Life is a Miracle*, is that to care about the planet requires not just an intellectual acknowledgement of the importance of the "world's multitude of places and creatures," but also an imaginative response to their beauty. Beauty cannot be fully apprehended by the intellect; it must be internalized: "To know imaginatively is to know intimately, particularly, precisely, gratefully, reverentially, and with affection" (138). How can we as a species hope to save our planet unless we care for its places and creatures with our hearts and not just our minds? At present, our schools do a poor job of both. They neglect the imagination even more than the mind. It is a tragic neglect.

And, third, our unawareness of beauty and neglect of the imagination is compounded by education systems which are just that, systems. They are systems designed to produce, even mass produce, conformity, what J.P. Guilford called "convergent thinking." Standardized tests require convergent thinking. There is only one answer to any given question that students are trained to regurgitate. Reductive thinking is encouraged. One person designs a question and thereafter every test-taker is trained to try to figure out what the test-designer wants for an answer. Creative responses to standardized tests are fatal. So, as our educational establishment seeks to impose "standards" and high-stakes tests on the system, the arts become more and more valuable counter measures. For the power of the arts is that it encourages, even requires divergent thinking. The arts demand that each artist express his or her own feelings and creative apprehension of the world.

Our schools try to explain things. Yet, as Berry reminds us, "The only things really explainable are explanations." What can ultimately be explained? Only things which have defined limits. "Explanation is reductive, not comprehensive; most of the time when you have explained something, you discover leftovers. An explanation is a bucket, not a well" (113).

So the arts combat ugliness, insensitivity to the world, and standardized-reductive thinking. This is why they must be preserved. The world's preservation depends upon their preservation.

"All I'm saying is, giving a little something to the
arts might help our image."

REFERENCES:

Abrams, David. 1995. *The Spell of the Sensuous*. New York: Pantheon Books.

Berman, Morris. 2000. *The Twilight of American Culture*. New York: W.W. Norton & Company.

Berry, Wendell. 2000. *Life is a Miracle*. Washington, D.C.: Counterpoint.

Cluthey, Rick. 1965. *The Cage*. (Out of print: Available through the author.)

Cummins, Paul F. and Anna Cummins. 1998. *For Mortal Stakes: Solutions for Schools and Society*. Las Vegas and New York: Bramble Books and Peter Lang Publishing.

Dillard, Annie. 1982. *Teaching A Stone to Talk*. New York: Harper & Row.

Ghiselin, Brewster, ed. 1952. *The Creative Process*. New York: Mentor Books.

Guilford, J.P. 1967. *The Nature of Human Intelligence*. New York: McGraw-Hill.

Lewis, C.S. 1947. *The Abolition of Man*. New York: The Macmillan Co.

Upchurch, Carl. 1996. *Convicted in the Womb*. New York: Bantam Books.

Urgo, Joseph R. 2000. *In The Age of Distraction*. New York: Random House.

> *When the cannons have stopped firing, and the great victories of finance are reduced to surmise and are long forgotten, it is the art of the people that will confront future generations. The arts do more to sustain the peace than all the wars, the armaments and the threats and the warnings of the politicians.*
> — Arthur Miller, 2002

CHAPTER ELEVEN

New Roads School:
Where Diversity Meets Inclusion

"There is no use trying," said Alice; "one can't believe impossible things."
I dare say you haven't had much practice," said the Queen. "When I
was your age, I always did it for half an hour a day. Why, sometimes
I've believed as many as six impossible things before breakfast."
— Lewis Carroll

What you want to do is make noise,
trouble and change.
— Charles Bowden

New Roads School in Santa Monica, Calif. disproves the old adage "there is nothing new under the sun," for New Roads is a relatively new combination of ingredients even in the world of new schools. Created in 1995, the independent school is a unique blend of: a) a strong commitment to diversity, inclusion, and social justice in its mission and its curriculum; b) innovative and path-breaking approaches to creating facilities; c) a private school with an extensive commitment to serving the public school community; and, finally, d) leadership in several substantial reform movements and curricular innovations. Any one of the above four ingredients would call for attention and, perhaps, notoriety, but the combination of all four has resulted in a new creation under the sun.

The road leading to New Roads was, however, a bumpy one with several dead-ends and detours along the way. The first one came in 1993 when I tried to create a public-private school joint venture. My vision had been to take an under-utilized public school (Coeur d'Alene) campus (two-thirds asphalt) and to improve the entire campus, build new buildings, and double the size of the existing student body of a K–5 elementary public school for 200 students, adding 200 tuition paying students. At the time, public schools were receiving about $4,000 per student. I proposed adding 200 private school students who would pay $10,000 each. The combined funds would thus have enabled us to spend $7,000 per pupil. In effect, the private school tuitions would provide a $3,000 boost, or subsidy, for the existing school children. A great deal? You would think, but the teacher's union declared war on the idea, and I was forced to abandon it.

Nevertheless, my goal remained constant, to create a truly diverse school which would bring together children from all racial, ethnic, economic, cultural and national groups to work, to teach, to learn to respect each other, and to value and celebrate diversity. With the public school system unwilling to break the mold (most of the LAUSD schools are de facto segregated schools), I was forced to go back to what I knew: the creation of a new campus exclusively for our private school.

The first step (1994) was to design a foundation dedicated to creating new schools. We named this agency the New Visions Foundation, and New Roads School was its first venture. I gathered together a few colleagues from other ventures, and we quickly created our non-profit corporation based on several principles. First, we decided that a New Visions school would require diversity: diversity of students and parents, teachers and administrators, trustees and advisors, and diversity within the curriculum itself. Second, we determined that our schools must reflect a commitment to social justice and to environmental sanity.

To guarantee our pledge to diversity, we even wrote into our by-laws a requirement that a "New Visions School" would consist of a minimum of 40% non-white students.

Actually, we spent two hours at one board meeting discussing whether it should be a 40% "students of color" or "minority" or "non-white" or whatever. At one point, a Korean woman to my left and a Latino man to my right placed their arms next to mine and said, "What color are we?" In reality, our "colors" were indistinguishable. At which point our African-American president of the board said, "If you were my color, you would know the full import of color in America." He said that he had the education, background, training, ability and experience to move in just about any circle, but he lacked the one thing that had prevented him from full access to the higher orders of power. He lacked "skin privilege." It was a stunning comment.

In any event, the New Visions Foundation hammered out a philosophy statement that is, I believe, rather unusual in its honesty and depth. In addition, it is truly the yardstick by which the school measures its growth and activities. Here it is:

> The goal is diversity and balance. The categories become confusing, extraordinarily complex, and categorization itself is, to many people, demeaning and disrespectful. Yet it is clear that our society has created hierarchical and exclusive opportunities based upon skin color, names, facial characteristics, addresses, gender, occupations and wealth. The goal of the New Visions Foundation/New Roads School is to assist young people as they strive to transcend these barriers and restrictions by providing quality educational opportunities for children regardless of how society categorizes them. It is the barriers and restrictions that are the enemies to a progressive society, not the categories of diversity.
>
> Therefore, the New Visions Foundation/New Roads School is seeking a student population which would encompass the broadest possible range of cultural, racial, religious, ethnic, economic and national categories. Further, to the extent that societal discrimination has placed economic disadvantages upon people of certain backgrounds, the school would use its economic resources to provide the financial assistance that would allow students of these backgrounds to attend.
>
> The intent and goal of this board is clear. We seek an equitable distribution of opportunities in our society and we believe a quality education is a road to that end. We seek a community rich in its variety of contributions from every gender, race, culture, language, sexual orientation, nationality, religion, and whatever other categories may emerge in the future. Philosophically we do not like the idea of quotas, but we recognize that our country is racially and economically divided and, therefore, that we are committed to achieving a student body of a minimum of 40% students "of color" with no group representing more than 60% of the total, and ideally, with no one racial group representing a predominance. The ultimate goal is to produce graduates who will be leaders of excellence, imagination, creativity and moral fitness to guide this next generation as it navigates in a diverse and inclusive world.

As the school founders were designing the philosophy, some curriculum ideas, marketing plans and recruitment strategies, and the all important question of *where* came up. Where would the school be located? Necessity, and even desperation, is indeed often the mother of creation. Because New Roads was planned to forgo approximately 50% of its potential income as financial aid, it was clear that we could not afford an expensive rent. Also, we had no initial funds to purchase a campus. Clearly we needed a low-rent facility. However, we also needed to locate our campus where the 50% who could pay tuition of nearly $12,000 the first year would be willing to place their children. The campus could not be located in a "low-rent" neighborhood, yet we needed a low rent. We determined to seek a shared-use space. A quick search led us to the Santa Monica Boys and Girls Club — serving primarily an after-school, public school population. We met with Allan Young, one of the truly superb administrators of Boys and Girls Clubs nationally, and we arranged to raise the funds to renovate his building for school use and to lease the space from 8:00a.m. — 3:00p.m. Since many of our children had single moms or both parents worked, the students could stay until 5:00 or 6:00 p.m. utilizing the Boys and Girls Club's after-school programs. The club came with an indoor gymnasium and two outdoor playgrounds, and the rent was and remains affordable and reasonable.

Having secured the lease with Allan Young's Boys and Girls Club and having already begun a student recruitment drive, we hired our first head of school to whom my assistant, Adrienne McCandless, and I turned over the recruitment of students and faculty. David Bryan was my choice and enthusiastically seconded by our Board of Directors to be our Head. A former lawyer and teacher, and Dean of the Human Development department at Crossroads School, David offered a rare combination of right and left brain intelligence, creativity and imagination mixed with a rigorous attention to detail. Significantly, David embodies the values of kindness, warmth and sensitivity to other's feelings as well as a passion for social justice and ecology. He remains, we all believe, the perfect Head for our school and the school's quick success (a positive city-wide image within five years) is directly attributable to David.

In September of 1995, less than 12 months from the time we determined to create the school, New Roads opened its (actually, opened the Boys and Girls Club) doors to 70 6th, 7th, and 8th grade students. The first year went remarkably smoothly and we kept our

9th grade at the Club for the school's second year. When the 9th became 10th, we arranged for what we thought would be a long-term relationship with Santa Monica College. We were to be a kind of lab school within their campus. However, no sooner had we begun fall classes there for our 9th and 10th grade students than the college decided they needed the space (4 classrooms and a mini-office), and we would have to evacuate in June.

Perhaps I should have learned my Coeur d'Alene lesson, but in seeking a new campus I ventured again into the public-private, joint-venture arena. My idea was to utilize under-used public school space for the mutual benefit of a public school and a private school. By 1997, New Roads School had a high school of grades 9 and 10. We rented space for our classes on a year-to-year lease, but wanted a more permanent arrangement. I approached a local public elementary school principal, Yuri Hyashi, who administered Walgrove School, a 10+ acre campus, about seven acres of them unused, cracked, weed-infested asphalt. My idea was that New Roads would enter into a long-term (i.e., 50 years) lease with the Los Angeles Unified School District (LAUSD) and build our high school on the back third of the property. We also promised the following:

- To bear all costs of the renovation;

- To "green" the entire 10 acres: surround it with trees, create gardens for the students, landscape the campus, etc.;

- To build a full soccer field on the middle third of the campus — to be used by Walgrove Elementary, New Roads, and the surrounding community (soccer fields in Los Angeles are in great demand);

- To have our high school students (all college bound — also a diverse group) tutor the elementary children one-on-one, approximately three hours per week. The elementary teachers thought this an immensely exciting prospect;

- To remodel the existing tiny auditorium into an expanded, more efficient, and beautiful place for children and for community use;

- ◆ To raise funds to connect the elementary school's five bungalow classrooms for Special Education Children into a full center for special education;

- ◆ To architecturally tie the elementary school into the high school design, thus making it more aesthetically pleasing to all.

All this I estimated at around eight to ten million dollars, and I believed we could raise the funds because the concept was new, innovative, and a win-win design.

The principal, the faculty, and the neighborhood (1000 signed a petition endorsing it) loved the plan. And the Los Angeles Unified School District? Once again, the idea was too far out of the box. They ran me from committee to committee, stalled, delayed, and postponed a decision to the point that I had to make other plans or see New Roads evaporate.

Finally, after giving me the runaround for eight months, the Board of Education voted to move another public school on to the back half of the property. The vote was clearly a way of avoiding the public-private joint venture. Now, five years after the vote, (March of 2004), nothing has happened with the property, and it is still two-thirds cracked, weed-covered asphalt.

Gradually, as I saw that the LAUSD-Walgrove campus idea was going nowhere, I realized we had a desperate situation: Where would the school be located in the coming year? We sought deals at one place after another and nothing seemed to work. And on July 1, 1999, I received a telephone call from the school Head, David Bryan, who said, "Paul, it's not that I'm panicking, but we have a 9–10–11th grade group of parents and students who want to know where, and even if, school is going to be in September." I mumbled something about, "don't worry, we'll find something." But I was in a state of high anxiety. Fortunately, I heard via the grapevine that another private school was moving out of a prime location. I called the landlord and at the 11th hour (July 30, 1999) we were able to sign a lease for a small campus — one U-shaped building, surrounding a tiny courtyard in an increasingly popular and valuable commercial corridor of West Los Angeles. There is an old saying that God protects fools and drunks. Well, I certainly wasn't drunk. . . . Having dodged the bullet, we had 27 days to get ready for our ninth, tenth and eleventh grade students to arrive.

Turning back a moment to the time that the 9th grade became 10th, we were determined to start yet another middle school. Typically, when families from underserved neighborhoods seek a quality college-preparatory private school for their children, they must trek across town to higher income neighborhoods where the "white folks" have established their "elitist" schools. The New Visions Foundation decided to establish a quality private school in a predominantly African-American populated neighborhood and we hoped we could also attract white, Latino and Asian families due to our school's reputation.

In searching for our campus, we focused on an economically diverse minority neighborhood, an area known as Baldwin Hills, which consists primarily of lower, middle and upper economic classes of African-American families. We heard of a Baha'i Temple that was planning to remodel one wing of its building into a community center. We met with the Los Angeles Baha'i Center and suggested that they remodel the space into a school (grades 6–7–8) and rent it to us during the day, while they could use the space after 6:00pm Monday-Friday, Saturdays, Sundays, and summers for their community center. They agreed and, once again, we entered into a shared-use agreement that we hoped would be a win-win program for each organization.

To my great disappointment, and, I confess surprise, the Baldwin Hills campus project failed financially. Ironically, it was a big educational success — the parents, teachers and students saw the school-campus as a jewel. It had small classes, a high shared morale, wonderful teachers, and parents who saw their children, many for the first time, loving school and fully engaged in the process. The problems were financial.

When we launched this private school in a predominantly black neighborhood, I believed that we could attract upper-middle and upper class African-Americans as well as whites in surrounding vicinities, some of whom would be able to pay from half to full tuition. We did not attract any! Those who could pay continued sending their children across town to the existing prestigious, predominantly white schools rather than take a chance on a brand new school in their own neighborhood. Perhaps these families were looking us over to see if we would survive and flourish, but while they waited (if in fact, they waited) we lost money, over $1.5 million dollars after five years. Finally, at the end of the fourth year, we had to face reality: a) the school had the exact same enrollment as the first year (52); b) of the 52 students only two paid full tuition; c) we were losing over $300,000 a year compared to the other two campuses; d) there was no end in sight to the process. Consequently, the Board of Trustees voted to close the campus at the end of the fifth year when our lease expired at the Baha'i Temple (June 2002).

Sadly, I reviewed several miscalculations. One was the financial assessment of who could and would pay $12,000 a year in tuition. Another was trying to impose an idealistic vision *upon* the community, without a strong base of support to launch the school. We launched it first and then tried to persuade the community to join us. When I helped to create another charter school in a low income neighborhood, it succeeded — because the community invited us first.

Postscript:

In spite of my sense of failure at the closing of the second middle school campus, the story doesn't end here. In fact, there is a happy ending. New Roads Baldwin Hills was led during its five years by a wonderful African-American woman who had previously been an English teacher in the inner city trenches. Charletta Johnson is an articulate, passionate, compassionate, and effective leader. When she saw that the campus was not financially viable, she began making plans for starting a brand new charter school. She credits New Roads as being her model on many counts. The obvious first count is the example that starting a new school is possible. But beyond that, Charletta asserts that New Roads taught her that an entire school can be a warm, nurturing place with a rich, diverse curriculum. So in September of 2002, arising from its ashes like the phoenix, Charletta's creation was born: The Community Harvest Charter School, a middle school of 160 students will add a grade each year until it is a 6–12 school. Community Harvest is a wonderful venture with many former New Roads teachers on staff and with an inspired Charletta at the helm.

As of September 2002, New Roads School operated two campuses: The West Los Angeles (Olympic Boulevard site) grades 9–12 (on 1.2 acres) and the Santa Monica Boys and Girls Club campus, grades 6–7–8.

This is the short-form story of the creation of the three and then two campuses. The story of the daily life at each school is another matter. First of all, it must be said that the diversity helped create a wonderful community where differences are respected and even honored. Our fully integrated school is working and students are not just sorting themselves out into racial cliques. There is some racial grouping, but it is not the dominant factor in the community.

In addition to its commitment to diversity, New Roads School seeks to imbue its students with a passion for social justice. From the very names of world leaders and heroes on the classroom doors (rather than numbers, we name rooms after such figures as Zapata, Menchu, Zinn, Aung San Suu Kyi, Huerta, Chomsky, Chavez, etc.) to the weekly two-hour workshops on social justice and environmental issues, New Roads holds true to its founding philosophy. The workshops are, perhaps, the curricular key to this quest. In each workshop — a weekly, two-hour, team-taught (three or four teachers) class — students are engaged in discussions, activities, and projects dealing with issues such as:

Prejudice and bias
Rights of the disabled
Endangered Species
Child labor
Animal rights
Using art in activism
AIDS
Ecological design
Consumerism
Poverty and privilege

The essence of the workshop is to bring issues to each student's consciousness and to activate their inherent sense of fairness. We believe that young people have a deep sense of what is and what is not fair. Thus, for example, issues of huge global disparities of wealth among individuals and nations will often lead students to ask the all important questions of why? and what can be done about this?

Similarly, we seek to arouse students' curiosity, interest, and, ultimately, indignation about the rapid depletion of their ecological heritage, the Earth, by the forces of consumerism and corporate profit. The workshops on ecology and environmental sanity are designed not to frighten students, but to help them learn to care and to seek ways to undo damage in their lives and to prevent further degradation of our beautiful planet and all its unique resources. The administration and the faculty take great care to make the workshops hopeful.

Originally the workshop was designed to be a service learning class. So often school community service is thought of by students as meeting their hourly requirements by "doing good." Some students are able to see beyond compiling hours to meet their obligations, but many just want to get their hours done. The theory behind Workshop is that service and the desire to take action would grow out of an on-going exploration of an issue.

The latest plan at New Roads is to create a Community Action major in the high school. Students in academic classes will also be teaching assistants in some Workshop classes and also help organize Workshop days. In addition, high school students have already begun creating Workshop presentations for middle school students.

So far, the response from students is encouraging. Many say the Workshop period is their most valued class each week. The ultimate measurement will lie somewhere in the future; that is, how much each student will do in his or her life to be actively part of the ecological solution rather than a continuation of the problem. We do hope, moreover, to see our graduates become involved in environmental causes either vocationally or as concerned-active citizens. Our article of faith is that consciousness precedes action and that passionate role models, such as David Bryan and the faculty, will have a deep impact on students.

What lies ahead for New Roads School? Many exciting ventures. For one, New Roads recently (July 1, 2003) merged with and absorbed an elementary school (formally Newbridge School) and plans to bring the elementary, middle, and high school together on the new Herb Alpert Educational Village, scheduled to open in September of 2006. Second, moving more deeply into the arena of full inclusion (discussed in the next chapter). Third, developing sister school relationships with two schools in Japan, which may even lead to the creation of a New Roads branch in Tokyo and/or Kyoto. Already we have a flourishing two-way exchange program with a school in Northern Japan. Fourth, developing a film institute at the New Roads campus for our students and for inner-city and low-income students nearby. The institute would offer classes in film history and aesthetics, screen writing; film-making; editing; marketing; and other related courses. The classes are planned as joint ventures with film studios and major film figures.

One thing is certain: New Roads is committed to growth, change, and openness to new ideas. We hope that our very name will be a constant reminder of our identity.

DISTRACTION	VIOLENCE	CONSUMERISM	MONEY
ENTERTAINMENT	GREEDINESS	INDUSTRIALISM	POSITION
BANALITY	CORRUPTNESS	MATERIALISM	PRESTIGE
TRIVIALITY	PROFIT	SPEED	POWER
	MOTIVATED		
VULGARITY		COMFORT	
LIQUIDATE THE		GADGETRY	
ENVIRONMENT			
FOR PROFIT			

CONFORM
ADJUST
FIT IN

EDUCATION

OUTSIDE THE BOX:
THE REAL GOALS OF EDUCATION

"To sort the trivial from the significant." — Virgo

"To create conditions in which the students should be able to think and act fearlessly." — Laia Sain Das

"To learn for the hell of it." — Abbie Hoffman

"To learn how to live in the spirit of play rather than work."
— Alan Watts

"To Help the individual to perceive the enduring values of life."
— Krishnamurti

CHAPTER 12

The Educational Village:
Integrative, Inclusive, Interactive

*All of us do not have equal
talents but all of us should
have an equal opportunity to
develop our talents.*
— John F. Kennedy

*Meaning is a blind god
who limps through the actual world
seeking any attachment
looking for good company.*
— Chris Wallace-Crabbe
By and Large

All across America children and adults are segregated from one another. They are segregated by race and economics (often closely related); by ethnic groups and national identities — in Los Angeles, for example, there is a Little Tokyo, a Jewish-Russian neighborhood, a Chinatown, a Koreatown, and so on. They are also separated by learning modalities — consequently we have various special education schools where non-neurologically typical (NNT) children are segregated from neurologically typical kids (NTs). Even if they are on the same campus, NNTs and NTs are usually sequestered from each other. In addition, generations are segregated — children move away from home and seniors and grandparents are sent off to their own habitats. Not only do we segregate generations and ethnic-national groups from each other, more and more people are living in gated tracts and homes protected by private police. In fact, there are more private than public police today in America. The sad consequences of various kinds of segregation range from simple obliviousness to active hostility and violence. Conventional thought states that familiarity breeds contempt. However, we believe that familiarity often leads to greater understanding, tolerance, respect, and sometimes even true community.

A further unfortunate consequence of these various forms of segregation in education is that the adults, teachers, administrators, parents, and specialists are also separate, and hence often do not interact and learn from one another. As a result, racial nuances, modes of teaching, cultural variances and subtleties are not shared, while monochromatic perceptions of the world persist. Add to this the insidious trend toward cultural homogenization and we find the peculiar phenomenon of some groups remaining isolated from each other while their very diversity is being eroded by the mass-consumerist-materialism of the Western, particularly the American, world.

To address at least some of these issues, the New Visions Foundation, a small group of educational reformers in California, has designed The Herb Alpert Educational Village to bring together an assorted group of students and non-profit organizations, each in its turn dedicated to diversity, inclusion, and interaction.

Creating collaborations of non-profits through the sharing of physical space is an exciting and relatively new concept. For example, the Thoreau Center for Sustainability and Fort Mason, both located in San Francisco, are sites where multiple non-profits share space in buildings that would otherwise have been vacant. Currently, several non-profits across the country are looking to launch their own collaboratives in order to secure space at lower rent and as a byproduct, promote their own longevity.

The New Visions' design is, however, somewhat different. Our design takes the concept of collaboration beyond just the sharing of space. Instead, though still within the framework of offering lower than market-rate rents, the Village will focus on bringing together educational non-profits in *both physical and philosophical collaborations* in order to encourage symbiotic relationships to benefit pre-school through twelfth grade education. The Village will be a unique collaboration as well as a national model of structuring new paths of delivering educational services as well as encouraging new ways of thinking about education. Primarily, we plan to integrate three principles that too often are separate in our schools. The Village hopes to combine these elements seamlessly:

1. *Inclusivity* — We plan to open our pre-school (and by extension, a New Roads Elementary School) to *all* children, ranging from those with severe learning problems to the highly gifted;

2. *Interactive* — We plan to have all our pre-K through 12 students

collaborating on tutorials, apprenticeships, one-on-one teaching, and independent projects; and

3. *Diversity* — The New Visions Foundation and New Roads School are committed to incorporating the highest degree of diversity — racial, economic, cultural and ethnic, international, and, now, learning differences in their program and investigating the best educational practices.

The various partners of this Village (on approximately two-and-a-half acres) will include:

- an existing elementary, middle and high school, known collectively as New Roads School;

- a new pre-school — inclusive;

- a "school within a schol" for special education children

- a dance academy — for "the Village" students and the public after school;

- a foundation sponsored library resource center;

- a foundation (M.I.N.D.) which promotes math understanding through piano keyboard programs;

- a community outreach program — The Bridge Program — providing free college credit courses in the humanities for marginalized adults living near the poverty level;

- a New Visions Foundation office to co-create and export film programs to inner city schools.

- a New Visions Foundation office, Center for Educational Opportunity, to place foster children in private schools;

- a foundation, The Charlie Foundation, promoting the ketogenic diet for pediatric epilepsy;

- a foundation, PS Arts, to restore the arts to public schools;

- a New Visions Foundation office, Friends for the Future, promoting international student exchanges;

◆ a New Visions Foundation office, Families Helping Families: families with means helping less fortunate households;

◆ our own New Visions Foundation offices;

◆ a foundation, The Early Childhood Parenting Center.

The central idea is that besides sharing space, these groups will design programs together, host conferences and workshops together, teach each other about their own areas of expertise and co-author articles and papers. Significantly, they will learn together by doing projects together. Our plans for the delivery of education can be illustrated by several specific examples:

1. The New Roads High School students will tutor the pre-school and elementary special ed children;

2. The M.I.N.D. Institute will provide their unique form of musical keyboard and math software instruction to the elementary and special ed students;

3. The various non profits will participate in ongoing roundtables where educational issues will be discussed from the perspective of each organization. From these discussions, topics for research, conferences, etc., can be established, such as: Educating the Public about Pediatric Epilepsy, New Educational Frontiers in Autism, Developing Educational Opportunities for Foster Children, The Role of the Arts in the Curriculum, and Leadership Training for Principals in the Twenty-First Century; and

4. A Film Institute will provide courses on campus for New Roads students and will export programs to inner-city schools, as well as providing summer classes for the wider community.

On the Village campus, we will share various facilities including a theater (350 seats), a library (with various relevant special collections), a gymnasium, and a coffee shop-faculty lounge — leadership center (to encourage the teachers and administrators from all the organizations to gather and create plans on a formal or informal basis).

At the heart of the Village is the notion, in microcosm, of modeling how the principles of diversity, inclusion, and interaction might come together. Each of these principles requires further discussion.

Diversity is a sort of motherhood principle — everyone is in favor of it. Yet, peculiarly, it rarely exists in our schools. There is, for example, a higher percentage of children attending segregated schools in 2002 than *before* the Brown vs. Board of Education decision of 1954. Whether or not it is intentional or historically accidental is debatable. Nevertheless, Los Angeles Unified School district is now 89.8% non-white, even though Los Angeles County is 48.7% white. Not only is there little diversity in many public and private schools, there is also segregation of a disproportional nature in prisons, where African Americans and Latinos represent a higher percentage of inmates.

We are a diverse, multicultural nation with a system of highly segregated schools. New Roads School in Santa Monica, California (see Chapter 11) is 50% non-white, and there is an almost equal percentage of African-Americans, Asians, and Latinos along with Caucasian students. This school, however, has set diversity as a key part of its mission. Without such an active commitment, intermingling will not happen. The social forces impeding integration can only be overcome by a deep determination to *not* let segregation occur.

I have always believed I valued diversity. A group of us founded Crossroads School in 1971, and we set in stone the policy that 10% of our operating budget would go to financial aid to help us achieve a mixed student population. This policy has enabled us to achieve about a 30% minority enrollment. Our 10% represents a big commitment: $2.5 million dollars of aid in 2002–03 off the top of a $25 million budget. Still, 70% of the students are white.

New Roads was founded upon the principle that a minimum of 40% of the student population should be non-white. We were determined to avoid being primarily a school for the white and the wealthy. At 50% non-white, we have achieved this goal, and because of this diversity, I believed that we could call ourselves an inclusive school. After all, we included in our school a racially and economically heterogenous population. However, when we admitted a student confined to a wheel chair with cerebral palsy, a student with Aspergers Syndrome, and several other students with substantial learning disabilities, I began to see how limited my own definition of inclusive had been. I read more carefully about the Individuals with Disabilities Education Act (IDEA — particularly the 1998 amendments), which lists thirteen categories of qualifying disabilities: autism, deafness, deaf-blindness, hearing impairment, mental retardation, multiple disabilities, orthopedic impairment, other health impairment, emotional disturbance, specific learning disability, speech or language impairment, traumatic brain injury, and visual impairment, including blindness. Over the years, I have had limited contact with such children and I quickly came to see that if we were to continue to use the word "community," then our Village must include the widest range of children.

Having been educated in private schools, both high school and college, and then teaching and administering in private schools for over forty years, I had simply been shielded from the world of special education. That public school children with disabilities are now mandated to be educated as much as possible with children who do not have disabilities had pretty much escaped my attention. But when such children attended Crossroads and New Roads, I came to see the value for everyone brought about by their inclusion. Furthermore, I came to learn that "a substantial body of research supports the effectiveness of inclusive practices for children with disabilities and children who are developing typically" (Cavallaro & Haney, p.22).

Coincidentally, my eyes were opened wider by two families already in our school community. One graduated with our first class of Crossroads School. Keith Resnick, class of 1976, and his wife, Leslie, had a daughter, Lili Claire. A few weeks after her birth she was diagnosed with Williams Syndrome.

Williams Syndrome is a neurogenetic birth defect which results in serious physical problems as well as severe to moderate mental retardation. It leaves one hemisphere of the brain devastated. Consequently, Williams children do not do well with linear thinking, mathematics, geometry, directions, and visual art. Yet surprisingly, they often have an acute sense of music and poetic language. Often they are happy, friendly, possessed with superb memories for people, and relatively innocent and unaware of danger. They can, however, function quite productively in society.

Lili Claire died when she was five and-a-half months old after undergoing an eighteen hour open-heart surgery to correct a severe heart condition that is common to Williams Syndrome. When I learned of Lili Claire and the foundation that Keith and Leslie created to honor their daughter, it occurred to me that their foundation would be a wonderful addition to our Village. The educators present would learn about Williams and the students would interact and learn from each other. Our music program, in particular, would be a place to bring the neurologically typical students in classroom relationships with Williams students.

The second family, Jim and Nancy Abrahams, had one son graduating from Crossroads and the other, Charlie, has a foundation named after him. I had received an appeal every year from the Charlie Foundation and dutifully sent in a small contribution to be polite, but I really didn't pay much attention to the foundation's mission. Then, one night, I caught the tail end of a late night movie on television entitled *First Do No Harm,* featuring Meryl Streep. I saw the credits and was startled to see Jim's name as producer. I soon called him to have coffee and tell me about the Foundation. We talked for over an hour and what Jim told me is presented in this condensed account:

On March 11, 1993, I was pushing my son, Charlie, in a swing when his head twitched and he threw his right arm in the air. The whole event was so subtle that I didn't even think to mention it to Nancy, my wife, until a couple of days later when it recurred. She said she had seen a similar incident. That was the beginning of an agony I am without words to describe.

Nine months later, after thousands of seizures, an incredible array of drugs, dozens of blood draws, eight hospitalizations, a mountain of EEGs, MRIs, CAT scans, and PET scans, one fruitless brain surgery, five pediatric neurologists in three cities, two homoeopaths, and countless prayers, Charlie's seizures were unchecked, his development "delayed," and he had a prognosis of continued seizures and progressive mental retardation.

Then, in December 1993, we learned about an obscure diet, consisting mainly of fat, for some kids with difficulty to control seizures. We took Charlie to Johns Hopkins, he started the diet, and since Christmas 1993, he has been seizure and drug free.

As a consequence of learning about the Lili Claire Foundation, the Charlie Foundation, Williams Syndrome and Pediatric Epilepsy, the idea of a Village began to take further shape. By bringing together various non-profits dealing with both neurologically typical and non-neurologically typical children, we could all support and learn from each other.

No sooner were such thoughts germinating than another area opened up to me. A friend of a Crossroads' Trustee came to see me about placing foster children in our schools. Deanne Shartin has had considerable experience with foster children and had located a philanthropist, Peter Morton, willing to underwrite five children — full tuition, counseling, tutoring, transportation — for them to attend private schools. We accepted four at New Roads School and the children, for the first time in their educational lives, have flourished. Here are accounts of their first year (The students names have been changed to ensure confidentiality).

A) For the first time in my life I have good friends to hang out with. Real friends. I don't know where my life would be if I hadn't gotten this chance to go to a really good private school. I never had a chance to really learn before because I kept having to go to new schools every time I got placed in another foster home. I felt so out of place in my last school. I never got involved in anything. But this last year I had a role in our school's production of *Fiddler on the Roof.* For the first time I can actually say my life is good.

— Jessie, 10th grader

B) Zena has been in foster care on and off since she was two-years-old and has had to face harsh things in her young life few of us can even begin to imagine. When she came to live with our family last year she was timid and hurt and angry. Being in a good private school has supported her inclination to achieve, provided real academic challenges for her, and is building up her self-esteem more than words can describe. Thanks to the New Visions Foundation, she's being shown avenues of opportunity bigger than her biggest dreams.

— foster parent of a 6th grader

C) Unfortunately, Dana didn't have good role models when she was younger. Now she's the one who's becoming a good role model for her younger brothers and sister. Getting a chance to attend one of the best private schools in town is making sure she's not only the first person in her family to graduate from high school, but that she's also going to be the first one to go to college. This girl will, I know, do great things for the world.

— foster parent of a 9th grader

D) CEO is like having a good parent who gets excited about things I do in school and doesn't want me to be worried about whether or not I'll be able to do stuff like the other kids, like getting to go on our class trip last spring, or having soccer shoes so I can play on the team, or getting this certain kind of calculator I needed this semester for algebra. I don't know how or why I got so lucky to get introduced to CEO, but I do know I feel blessed.

— Matt, 9th grader

Because of their success, the idea came to me to create a small organization dedicated to placing foster children in private schools all over southern California. Thus, we created the Center for Educational Opportunities (CEO) and hired Deanne to be our first Executive Director. CEO will have its office in our new Village complex and will be able to educate, along with the Lili Claire and Charlie Foundation, the various teachers, students, and administrators of the Village about foster children. As of September 2003, CEO has placed eighteen foster children in private schools and each is flourishing beyond our expectations. We hope to double the enrollment each year.

I have presided at over one hundred graduations (5th, 8th and 12th grades) during the past 32 years and perhaps the single most dramatic moment came in June of 2001 at the Crossroads 12th grade graduation. Eva was a student who had been at the school since 8th grade. She has cerebral palsy and is confined to a wheel chair. She was one of the graduation speakers and, at her moment in the program, was wheeled out by a friend in front of the several hundred members of the audience. Another friend stepped up to the podium and read the speech Eva had prepared. She composes by spelling on a communication board. Her speech was articulate, intelligent, and profoundly moving and, all the while it was being read, she smiled as her head and body jerked from side to side in the manner which makes most non-palsied people nervous and uncomfortable. With Eva, after a few moments her physical motions became matter-of-fact and her beauty of spirit and courage came into focus. In her speech, she recounted her early experiences at Crossroads:

> My first indication that things would go well was that Crossroads didn't hesitate about taking me on as a student. The administration and teaching staff were accommodating and willing to listen to my special needs. My amazing parents explained what cerebral palsy is to everybody who would listen — my teachers, the other students, the parents. They explained how I communicated, did my work, and took my tests. I think this introduction made everyone more comfortable, including me.
>
> Despite all that preparation, the kids found it difficult to relate to me at first. Nobody knew how to talk to someone who couldn't talk back in the conventional way. Eighth grade, my first year, was rough because most kids felt uncomfortable approaching me, and so I did my work but didn't really succeed socially. In ninth grade, things got a little easier. I wasn't such an oddity on campus because the kids had spent the previous year with me. A few brave souls took a risk and began interacting with me. That beginning had a snowball effect and slowly more and more kids would talk to me and I began to feel comfortable at Crossroads. The faculty, I think, was more at ease with me, too. My eighth grade teachers told my ninth grade teachers how I participated in class discussions and how I was able to complete my work. So, by the time I started ninth grade, my teachers were reassured that I could be part of their classes and be successful in them.
>
> Each grade in high school got increasingly better for me as I started to make friends. In my junior and senior years, different kids served as my in-class aides. As they learned about me, some of them became my really good friends.

She concluded by saying:

> Disability can be a difficult barrier to see beyond at first. But I hung in there and so did all my teachers, the administration, my counselors, and a large percentage of the kids. I believe that most people here see me and not my disability first. I now feel entirely part of the community.

Crossroads didn't let disability get in the way of educating as they would any other student. And that attitude matches my attitude about my disability, that it is part of who I am but not the only or not nearly the most important part of me. If Crossroads can see me so clearly, they can see other disabled students in the same way. My hope is that Crossroads will be open to more students with disabilities.

Her speech reinforced for me what I have come only recently to realize. We limit not only people with disabilities by segregating them from non-disabled people; we limit the non-disabled as well. It is not just that the non-disabled are denied opportunities to be helpful and to serve others, for this implies that the only kind of relationship possible is that of patronage and assistance. It overlooks the possibilities of genuine friendships and mutuality. Eva's courage is certainly instructive, but her basic intelligence and insights are of equal value. By including Eva in a private school that has had few severely disabled students, everyone grew and everyone at the school expanded their own sense of what is possible in life.

After meeting Keith and Leslie, Jim and Nancy, Deanne, Eva, and many others, it became clear to me and to the Head of New Roads School, David Bryan, that we should embrace full inclusion for our high school, our middle school, and our soon-to-be created elementary school in the Village.

We then began a series of meetings which brought together a long-time friend and mentor, Jack Zimmerman, with two founders of a family day care home who have made a commitment to join the Village with their pre-school, Pacific Children. These women, Hiroko Yokota and Maki Wakae, are also committed to full inclusion. Jack Zimmerman has a particular interest in autism (his granddaughter is autistic) and believes that:

These "special" children have truly become "canaries in the mines of our culture"; they are compelling, not only because we come to love them so much for who they are individually, but also because they are here to catalyze the expanded awareness needed to change our culture, and sooner rather than later.

> The vast and increasing numbers of autistic children are messengers reflecting critical imbalances in the ways we live our lives. In their silences and explosions of feeling, in the disruption of their biochemical makeup, in their obvious incompatibility with our established educational system and traditional medical paradigm, they are literally asking us to see how out of balance we have become, collectively and individually. They are a wake-up message, a desperate eleventh-hour call for us to realize the insanity of our priorities and the many dangers in our present courses of action (195).

What I have come to see is how limited my own vision was even though I have sometimes been called a visionary. We are already holding meetings of the various tentative and committed Village participants and I come away from each meeting learning more about what I don't know and more about the possibilities inherent in bringing together all our various groups.

Now having outlined our plans for the Village, I return to the title of this book, in particular, the subtitle: *Proceed With Passion: Engaging Students in Meaningful Education.* The question is: how will the Village engage students and help give them a sense of meaning and purpose? I think by now the answer to this question is apparent. Almost all of the proposed adventures between the village groups will place students in interactive, experiential relationships. They will tutor each other, act as peer counselors and apprentices, design joint programs and be given a variety of responsible roles in the co-designing and enactment of the Village. Students come alive when they are given responsibilities and when they can help each other. Passivity leads to boredom and alienation; activity gives them a sense of purpose. Furthermore, the variety of non-profits inhabiting the Village will open student's eyes to a wider range of potential college majors and career opportunities. In fact, the widening of career horizons is one of our goals. Social work, special education, community activism, environmental projects — these and a host of other areas will be part of the very air that the students breathe on the Herp Albert educational Village premises. When students watch television, they are indoctrinated with the notion that there are three careers possible — law, medicine, or police work. We believe the Village will demonstrate visibly and palpably that there are hundreds of exciting and meaningful careers in social, cultural, and community services. We also believe that the Village concept could be applied to public and private school campuses across the country.

Finally, we believe, that as John Kenneth Galbraith writes, in *The Good Society*: "To identify and urge the good and achievable society may well be a minority effort, but better that effort than none at all" (2). Dreams are exciting both in the design and the execution. By involving students in both, we give them the highest gift of education. The poet Wistawa Szymborska tells us "and whatever I do/will become forever what I've done." The key here is the doing. The Village will be committed to that which is essential for young people — and for which they hunger: doing something worthwhile.

REFERENCES:

Abrahams, Jim. 1997. Film: *First Do No Harm.* ABC-TV Movie.

Cavallaro, Claire C. and Michelle Henry. 1999. *Pre-school Inclusion.* Baltimore: Paul H. Brooks Publishing Co.

Cummins, Paul and Anna Cummins. 1998. *For Mortal Stakes: Solutions for Schools and Society.* New York: Peter Lang Publishing. Las Vegas, Nevada: Bramble Books.

Galbraith, John Kenneth. 1996. *The Good Society.* New York: Houghton Mifflin Co.

Rozsak, Theodore. 1973. *Where the Wasteland Ends.* New York: Anchor Books.

Szymborska, Wistawa. 1998. *Poems New and Collected.* New York: Harcourt.

Zimmerman, J.M. 2002. "Starving Brains, Starving Hearts, What Does It All Mean?" *Children with Starving Brains* by Jacquelyn McCandless. Las Vegas: Bramble Books [brambooks@att.net].

To Morrow to fresh woods, and pastures new.
— Milton, *Lycidas*

CONCLUSION I

Hope is joy in the presence of the future in the present.
— Barbara Cully, "Field Tone"

CONCLUSION I

The Engagement Process

Education is not the filling of a
pail, but the Lighting of a fire.
— Willam Butler Yeats

. . . Redeem
The time. Reedem
The unread vision in the higher dream . . .
—T.S. Eliot, *Ash Wednesday*

It is possible to engage students in their own education; to do so requires involving them in activity and subject matter that they find meaningful. Engagement and meaning are the twin pillars of a successful individual education and of a nation's school systems. Moreover, we have the knowledge of how to do this; we have resources and funds to make it happen. We lack the will, the consciousness and/or the leadership to take us down that fork in the educational road.

This book is a sort of blueprint, laying plans to revitalize our schools and enliven our students. Here is a brief summary of this blueprint. First, we need to attract teachers to the profession who have a passion for their subject matter and an ability to relate to their students. Furthermore, their salaries must be consistent with our rhetoric of the importance of teaching to our national well-being. We must also reassess the current obsessions with testing and accountability. An absorbed student will become self-accountable by virtue of involvement with the subject at hand, which no amount of testing can dictate. To achieve passionate engagement we must select books carefully and draw students into meaningful action and community-service projects. The curricular topics for study should be relevant to the students' lives and interests via multi-sensory and multi-intelligence learning modalities. The arts require a central position in the core curriculum. We must also treat education in a creative and playful manner.

What we teach is equally as important as how we teach. Social studies could be far more captivating if we were to balance and compare studying societies of the past with social issues found in our students' own neighborhoods. Juvenile delinquency — its causes and possible cures — will capture the interest of almost all teenagers with far greater intensity then the causes of the French Revolution or the social structure of the Aztecs. Studying social conditions of a local skid row, enhanced by a field trip to meet leaders of social agencies in lower income areas, will involve young students almost immediately.

Another subject of immediate concern to most students is a focus on the health of the planet itself. This study can begin on the campus of each school in America: what we do to harm or to benefit the environment of our schools. When students discover that the Earth is "our home," learning becomes more exciting. Consciousness not only precedes action, it engenders active learning and social action. Action itself is the way in which learning is solidified and made real. Thus, we begin with the school campus itself and proceed to local, national, and international issues of soil, water, animal life, air, food, species preservation and the like. When students realize that these issues affect everyone deeply, engagement is almost guaranteed.

Issues or problems of social justice combined with environmental crises inevitably lead to the political dimension. In an attempt to appear neutral and unbiased, schools typically avoid politics. This rarely works. Avoidance is a tacit vote for the status-quo, and of course, the status-quo is undoing the planet and its peoples. When schools find the courage to confront these issues, students will respond and become awake, aware, and involved. They know when their adult mentors, teachers, administrators, parents, are avoiding, and when they are dealing with, reality. Students respect adults who "walk the talk." A static, conformist education bores them, disheartens them, and leads many to drop out.

Consequently, educational leadership must examine more closely the issues of growing inequities of wealth, of degraded inner city conditions, of democracy versus plutocracy and oligarchy, of campaign financing, of placing business interests over environmental concerns, of media homogeneity and the neglect of dissent. Beyond these issues, we need to look at not just Paul Revere's ride or George Washington at the Potomac, sunny versions of national folklore, but also at the shadow side of American history. Students come alive when they sense that their teachers and school officials are not serving only bromides and approved versions of history, but are looking as well at the darkness that exists in all humans and in all institutions.

Such a look at American — and world — history requires an enormous amount of debate, discussion and even courage at every level of a school system, but it is possible. Where might such discussion lead? I offer one scenario as my second conclusion.

CONCLUSION II

WINDS FROM THE FUTURE

The Wind has changed;
it is time to go.
— Evan S. Connell

CONCLUSION II

Winds From The Future

Winds are coming from the future
With mysteriously beating wings.
— Nietzsche

The twentieth-century was arguably the most disastrous in human history. World wars, genocide, fratricide, global diaspora, extinction of species at an unprecedented rate — these describe the darkest few characteristics of that century. Past misconceptions, ideologies, and downright lies have largely created the on-going horrors of history. Unless we can recognize, examine, and reverse the patterns of the past, we will continue our reckless and self-defeating behaviors in the new century and beyond. The chief villains reappear century after century. They were worse in the 20th century because of the power which industry and technology have bestowed upon them. These villains are acquisitiveness, hierarchical dominance, classism, racism, genderism, and religious fanaticism. Expressed differently, they are oligarchy, totalitarianism, patriarchy, and theocracy. Furthermore, these villains are closely, if not incestuously, related to each other. Lust for acquisition has led both to imperialism and war, as well as to a global capitalist system in which fewer and fewer oligarchs and global corporations are amassing vaster and vaster wealth. Consequently, a worldwide social system consisting of a few very rich, a modest body of moderately well-off people, and growing hordes of poor, exploited, and desperate people is evolving. White men are by far the dominant lords of the world economy. Sadly, many religions around the world accommodate radical forces, maintaining their status-quo and preventing serious reform by fomenting hatred of other religions. As William Greider writes, "The world's great religions . . . still often reflect the tribalism that exalts faithful followers and demonizes the nonbelievers" (469).

For our students it is a depressing scenario. Furthermore, serious reform is obstructed not only by power structures outlined above, but by the histories and legends which govern and limit our ways of looking at the world. Our histories are generally apologies for existing systems. They are the stories of the winners — commissioned, written, and published *by* the winners. Consequently, the so-called losers' stories are not told, and they are, by default, defined as unimportant and useless. Thus, the assault upon, exploitation and subjugation of the poor by the rich is justified at every level of power.

Meanwhile, a new danger is becoming ever more threatening: the assault of man upon the Earth itself. The sagas of human progress and man's dominion over the Earth are largely responsible for this assault. The rape and destruction of the Earth is justified in the names of progress and transcendence. Capitalism-oligarchy-hierarchy all enable the few to exploit both other peoples and the planet they inhabit. Concurrently, the Judeo-Christian myth of human beings as caretakers of this Earth prior to ascending to greater rewards in heaven enables human beings to see themselves as "users" of the Earth rather than being interdependent creatures of the Earth. We have failed to see that our evolutionary uniqueness lies in our having evolved from the earth.

Nevertheless, all is not hopeless. We are "between stories," the old stories of our superiority over all and the new stories just emerging. We are awakening to the mysteriousness of the earth and acknowledging that somewhere within this mystery is our salvation. Planetary consciousness, interdependence, ecological awareness, and turning inward for guidance will bring the new stories into creation. There are already clear places to look for these "new" stories. Some are, in fact, old stories residing in traditions and religions of indigenous peoples who know how to live in harmonious relationship with the natural world, rather than seeing it as a resource to manage, exploit, and, ultimately eliminate for profit. Some new stories are offered by visionaries such as the Dalai Lama, Thomas Berry, and Gary Snyder. And Tom Hayden captures much of the wisdom we need for these new stories in his provocatively titled book, *The Lost Gospel of the Earth.*

New schools and new curricula will also help this process along, schools and curricula which will help students to liberate their thinking from the past in order to liberate the future from the prison of the past.

These new schools will offer curricula focusing upon the values of peaceful coexistence of humans with one another and of humans with nature. A planetary mysticism will help birth the new stories. Finally, the new visionaries will recognize and then enlighten others about the necessity of designing a more equitable distribution of the world's resources and opportunities. Clearly, some sort of world federation will be required to combat the increasing poverty and the growing global feudalism, as well as to halt the destruction and pollution of the Earth itself. We need to traverse beyond nations and United Nations to a United Species. Until now, history has been an unbroken series of patterns imposed upon the masses by the privileged few. To liberate the future from the chains of history will require the reversal of this pattern. The processes of examining these old patterns and imagining new stories should be exhilarating for students. They may learn that seeking and sometimes even finding meaning in their education is possible. If we proceed with passion toward this goal, our students will be fully engaged in their own education and we will all recover a sense of meaning, purpose, and joy in our lives.

BIBLIOGRAPHY

Part I – *The Search For Meaning*

⊬ Berman, Morris. 2000. *The Twilight of American Culture*. New York: W. W. Norton & Company.

Berry, Wendell. 2000. *Life Is A Miracle*. Washington, D.C.: Counterpoint.

Bruner, Jerome S. 1960. *The Process of Education*. New York: Vintage.

Buber, Martin. 1970. *I And Thou* (trans. by Walter Kaufmann). New York: Charles Scribner's Sons.

✓ Cummins, Paul and Anna Cummins. 1998. *For Mortal Stakes: Solutions for Schools and Society*. New York: Peter Lang Publishing, Inc.

Dewey, John. 1938. *Experience and Education*. New York: Touchstone.

Handy, Charles. 1998. *The Hungry Spirit*. New York: Broadway Books.

Kessler, Rachel. 2000. *The Soul of Education*. Alexandria, VA.: ASCD.

Kozol, Jonathan. 1995. *Amazing Grace: The Lives of Children and the Conscience of a Nation*. New York: Crown Publishers.

———. 2000. Ordinary Resurrections: Children in the Years of Hope. New York: Crown Publishers.

Krishnamurti, J. 1953. *Education and the Significance of Life*. San Francisco: Harper San Francisco.

———. 1974. *On Education*. England: Krishnamurti Foundation Trust.

Lantieri, Linda. 2001. *Schools With Spirit*. Boston: Beacon Press.

Lerner, Michael. 2000. *Spirit Matters*. Charlottesville, VA: Hampton Roads Publishing Company, Inc.

Levitt, Peter. 2003. *Fingerpainting on the Moon*. New York: Harmony Books.

Mohn, Reinhard. 2000. *Humanity Wins*. New York: Crown Business.

Merton, Thomas. 1953. *No Man Is An Island*. New York: Harcourt Brace & Co.

Miller, John P. 2000. *Education and the Soul.* New York (Albany), State University of New York Press.

Perinbanayagam, R.S. 1985. *Signifying Acts: Structure and Meaning in Everyday Life.* Carbondale: Southern Illinois University Press.

Roszak, Theodore. 1973. *Where the Wasteland Ends.* New York: Anchor Books.

Sohl, Robert and Audrey Carr, ed. 1976. *Games Zen Masters Play: Writings of R.H. Blyth.* New York: New American Library.

Watts, Alan. 1966. *The Book.* New York: Random House.

Whitehead, Alfred North. 1929. *The Aims of Education.* New York: The Macmillan Co.

Zimmerman, J.M. 2002. "Starving Brains, Starving Hearts, What Does It All Mean?" in: *Children With Starving Brains* by Jacquelyn McCandless. Las Vegas: Bramble Books.

How life lacks shape
Until it's given one by love.
— John Koethe

Part II – *A New Social Studies*

A Short-Idiosyncratic Bibliography

I)General

Barnasy, Frank Dr., General Editor. 1988. *The Gaia Peace Atlas.* (Forward by Javier Perez de Cuellar) [A challenging study of the prospects for peace on the planet.] New York: Doubleday.

Berman, Morris. 2000. *The Twilight of American Culture.* New York: W.W. Norton & Co.

Brown, Lester, et.al. 2001. *State of the World 2001.* [A Worldwatch Institute report on progress toward a sustainable society.] New York: W.W. Norton.

Diamond, Jared. 1992. *The Third Chimpanzee.* New York: Harper Perennial.

Galeano, Eduardo. 1987. *Memory of Fire.* [A three volume fictive historical trilogy of the Americas from the first native myths to modern times.] New York: W.W. Norton & Company.

Kane, Hal. 2001. *Triumph of the Mundane.* Washington, D.C.: Island Press.

II)A Sampling of Books About Indigenous People

Kane, Joe. 1996. *Savages.* New York: Vintage Books.

Rocha, Jan. 1999. *Murder in the Rainforest: The Yanomami, the Gold Miners and the Amazon.* [Describes the tragic cultural misunderstanding between the gold miners and the Yanomami, and analyzes the role of gold fever in the destruction of the Amazon rainforest and its indigenous peoples.] London: Latin American Bureau.

Henley, Paul. 1995. *Yanomami: Masters of the Spirit World.* [A unique heritage and wisdom of an endangered people.] San Francisco: Chronicle Books.

La Duke, Winona. 1999. *All Our Relations: Native Struggle for Land and Life.* Cambridge, Mass: South End Press.

Marcos, Subcomandante. 1999. *The Story of Colors.* El Paso, Texas: Cinco Puntos Press.

Mohawk, John C. 2000. *Utopian Legacies: A History of Conquest and Oppression in the Western World.* Santa Fe, New Mexico: Clear Light Publishers.

Thorpe, Dagmar. 2000. *People of the Seventh Fire.* [Presents the voices of twenty native community people — all involved in the complex work of cultural preservation and recovery of indigenous lifeways.] Ithaka: Akwe:kon Press.

III) Journals and Organizations

The Lannan Indigenous Peoples Program <http://www.lannan.org>.

Survival. [A worldwide organization supporting tribal peoples. It stands for their right to decide their own future and helps them protect their lives, lands and human rights.] 11–15 Emerald Street, London WC1N3QL. United Kingdom. (Tel: 0171–242–1441; Fax: 0171–242–1771).

Cultural Survival Quarterly. [Promotes the human rights, voices, and visions of indigenous peoples.] 215 Prospect St., Cambridge, MA 02139. (Tel: 617–441–5400; Fax: 617–441–5417; email: csinc@cs.org).

Native Americas: Hemispheric Journal of Indigenous Issues. Akwe:kon Press, American Indian Program, Cornell University, 450 Caldwell Hall, Ithaka, NY 14853 (Tel: 607–255–4308; Fax: 607–255–0185). Subscriptions: 1–800–9-native. Internet: <http://nativeamericas.aip.cornell.edu>

IV) Juvenile Education and Foster Children

Baca, Jimmy Santiago. 2001. *A Place to Stand*. New York: Grove Press.

Canada, Geoffrey. 1995. *Fist Stick Knife Gun*. Boston: Beacon Press.

Friedman, Terry B. et al. August 14, 2001. "Education Task Force Report" (on juvenile facilities in Los Angeles County). Los Angeles County Board of Education.

Humes, Edward. 1996. *No Matter How Loud I Shout: A Year in the Life of Juvenile Court*. New York: Touchstone.

Murphy, Patrick T. 1997. *Wasted: the Plight of America's Unwanted Children*. Chicago: Ivan R. Dee.

Parenti, Christian. 1999. *Lockdown America: Police and Prisons in the Age of Crisis*. New York: Verso.

Polakow, Valeria, ed. 2000. *The Public Assault on America's Children*. New York: Teachers College, Columbia University.

Romo Harriet D. and Toni Falbo. 1996. *Latino High School Graduation*. Austin: University of Austin Press.

Rose, Mike. 1989. *Lives on the Boundary*. New York: Penguin Books.

> *God shakes his fists eternally to say, /*
> *we're having more of yesterday today.*
> — B.H. Fairchild, "Weather Report"

Part III – *The Environment*

Ackerman, Diane. 1995. *The Rarest of the Rare: Vanishing Animals, Timeless Worlds.* New York: Random House.

Andrews, Richard N.L. 1999. *Managing the Environment, Managing Ourselves.* New Haven: Yale University Press.

Berry, Thomas. 1999. *The Great Work: Our Way into the Future.* New York: Bell Tower.

Bowden, Charles. 1995. *An Unnatural History of America.* New York: Random House.

Bowers, C.A. 1993. *Critical Essays on Education, Modernity, and the Recovery of the Ecological Imperative.* New York: Columbia University, Teachers College Press.

———. 1993. *Education, Cultural Myths, and the Ecological Crisis.* Albany: State University of New York Press.

Brown, Lester R. et al. 2003. *State of the World: 2003.* New York: Worldwatch Institute.

———. 2001. *Eco-Economy: Building An Economy for the Earth.* New York: W.W. Norton & Co.

Bullard, Robert D. ed. 1993. *Confronting Environmental Racism: Voices from the Grassroots.* Boston: South End Press.

Chertow, Marian & Daniel C. Esty, Eds. 1997. *Thinking Ecologically.* New Haven: Yale University Press.

Daedalus Magazine. Summer 1995. *The Liberation of the Environment.* Cambridge, MA: The American Academy of Arts and Sciences.

Davis, Wade. 1997. *One River: Explorations and Discoveries in the Amazon Rain Forest.* NewYork: Touchstone.

Earle, Sylvia A. 1995. *Sea Change: A Message of the Oceans.* New York: Fawcett Columbine.

Helvarg, David. 2001. *Blue Frontier: Saving America's Living Seas.* New

York: W.H. Freeman & Co.

Hill, Julia Butterfly. 2000. *The Legacy of Luna: The Story of a Tree, a Woman, and the Struggle to Save the Redwoods.* San Francisco: Harper Collins.

Little, Charles. 1995. *The Dying of the Trees: The Pandemic in America's Forests.* New York: Viking.

Matthiessen, Peter. 2001. *The Birds of Heaven: Travels with Cranes.* New York: North Point Press.

McKibben, Bill. 1995. *Hope, Human and Wild.* St. Paul, MN: Hungry Mind Press.

Orr, David W. 1994. *Earth in Mind: On Education, Environment, and the Human Prospect.* Washington, D.C.: Island Press.

Outwater, Alice. 1996. *Water: A Natural History.* New York: Basic Books.

Robbins, Ocean & Sol Solomon. 1994. *Choices for Our future.* Summertown, Tennessee: Book Publishing Co.

Schmidt, Ralph. 1999. *Forests to Fight Poverty.* New Haven: Yale University Press.

Shiva, Vandana. 2002. *Water Wars: Privatization, Pollution, and Profit.* Cambridge, MA: South End Press.

Suzuki, David. 1997. *The Sacred Balance.* Vancouver: Greystone Books.

Wilson, Edward O. 1992. *The Diversity of Life.* New York: W.W. Norton & Co.

Ocean Bibliography

Algalita Marine Research Foundation, 2001. *Our Synthetic Sea: Plastics in the Open Ocean* (Documentary).

Carson, Rachel L. 1951. *The Sea Around Us.* New York: Oxford University Press.

Cousteau, Jacques Yves. 1953. *The Silent World.* New York: Harper.

Earle, Sylvia. 1995. *Sea Change: A Message of the Oceans.* New York: Fawcett Columbine.

Ellis, Richard. 2003. *The Empty Ocean: Plundering the World's Marine Life.* Washington D.C.: Island Press.

Jackson, Jeremy. 1997. "Reefs Since Columbus" Coral Reefs 16 (suppl.):S23–S32.

Jackson, J.B.C. et al. 2001. "Historical Overfishing and the Recent Collapse of Coastal Ecosystems." Science 293: 629–638.

Helvarg, David. 2001. *Blue Frontier: Saving America's Living Seas.* New York: WH Freeman and Company.

Pauly, D. 1995. "Anecdotes and the Shifting Baseline Syndrome of Fisheries." *Trends in Ecology and Evolution* 10 (10) 430.

Rogers, Raymond A. 1995. *The Oceans Are Emptying: Fish Wars and Sustainability.* New York: Black Rose Books.

Safina, Carl. 1997. *Song for a Blue Ocean.* New York: Henry Holt

Website reference: Shifting Baselines <http://www.shiftingbaselines.org>

> *When poisons become fashionable, they do not cease to kill.*
> — C.S. Lewis

> *The Greatest beauty is organic wholeness,*
> *The wholeness of life and things,*
> *The divine beauty of the universe.*
> *Love that, not man apart from that . . .*
> — Robinson Jeffers

Part IV – *Politics and Education*

Allen, James, et al. 2000. *Without Sanctuary*. Santa Fe, New Mexico: Twin Palms Publishers.

Berry, Wendell. 1990. *What Are People For?* San Francisco: North Point Press.

Boggs, Carl. 2000 *The End of Politics: Corporate Power and the Decline of the Public Sphere*. New York: The Guilford Press.

Chomsky, Noam. 2000. *Chomsky on MIS-Education*. Lanham, Maryland: Rowman & Littleford Publishers.

Croteau, David and William Hoynes. 1994. *By Invitation Only: How the Media Limit Political Debate*. Monroe, ME: Common Courage Press.

Cuban, Larry and Dorothy Shipps. 2000. *Reconstructing the Common Good: Coping With Intractable American Dilemmas*. Stanford: Stanford University Press.

Danaher, Kevin, ed. 1996. *Corporations Are Going To Get Your Mama*. Monroe, ME: Common Courage Press.

Diamond, Jared. 1997. *Guns, Germs, and Steel: The Fates of Human Societies*. New York: W.W. Norton.

Ehrenreich, Barbara. 2001. *Nickel and Dimed: On (Not) Getting By In America*. New York: Metropolitan Books.

Freire, Paulo. 1990. *The Pedagogy of the Oppressed*. New York: Continuum.

———. 1996. *In Breaking Free: The Transformative Power of Critical Pedagogy*, ed. Pepi Leistyna, et.al. Cambridge, MA: *Harvard Educational Review*.

Gale, Kate & Charles Rammelkamp, eds. 2002. *Fake-City Syndrome; American Cultural Essays*. Los Angeles: Red Hen Press. (Includes an essay, "The Vital Left" by Paul Cummins).

Hacker, Andrew. 1992. *Two Nations: Black and White, Separate, Hostile, Unequal*. New York: Balantine books.

Kagan, Robert. 2003. *Of Paradise and Power.* New York: Random House.

Kozol, Jonathan. 1991. *Savage Inequalities.* New York: Harper Perennial.

Loewen, James W. 1995. *Lies My Teacher Told Me.* New York: Touchstone.

Nieto, Sonia. 2000. *Affirming Diversity.* (3rd edition) New York: Longman.

Parenti, Michael. 1983. *Democracy for The Few.* New York: St. Martin's Press.

Rorty, Richard. 1997. *Achieving Our Country.* Boston: Harvard University Press.

Roy, Arundhati, 2001. *Power Politics.* Cambridge, Massachusetts: South End Press.

Schell, Jonathan. 1998. *The Gift of Time: The Case for Abolishing Nuclear Weapons.* New York: Henry Holt.

Shorris, Earl. 1997. *New American Blues: A Journey Through Poverty to Democracy.* New York: W.W. Norton & Company.

Vidal, Gore. 1993. *The Decline and Fall of the American Empire.* Berkeley, CA: The Odonian Press.

———. 2002. *Dreaming War.* New York: Thunder's Mouth Press.

Some men see things as they are and ask why?
I dream things that never were and ask, why not?
— Robert F. Kennedy

Nations Confronting Their Shadow

Bly, Robert. 1998. *A Little Book on the Human Shadow.* San Francisco: Harper and Row.

Brown, Dee. 1971. *Bury My Heart at Wounded Knee.* New York: Holt, Rinehart & Winston.

Churchill, Ward. 1997. *A Little Matter of Genocide: Holocaust and Denial in the Americas 1492 to the Present.* San Francisco: City Lights Books.

Chomsky, Noam. 1994. *Secrets, Lies and Democracy.* Tucson, AZ: Odonian Press.

———. 1993. *Rethinking Camelot: JFK, The Vietnam War, and U.S. Political Culture.* Boston: South End Press.

———. 1991. *Terrorizing the Neighborhood.* San Francisco: Pressure Drop Press.

Cummins, Paul. 2001. *Keeping Watch: Reflections on American Culture, Education and Politics.* 1st Books Library <http://www.1stbooks.com>.

Forché, Carolyn. ed. 1993. *Against Forgetting: Twentieth Century Poetry of Witness.* New York: W.W. Norton and Company.

Freud, Sigmund. 1930. *Civilization and Its Discontents.* New York: W.W. Norton.

Galbraith, John Kenneth. 1996. *The Good Society.* New York: Houghton Mifflin Co.

Galeano, Eduardo. 1990. *Upside Down* (trans. by Mark Fried, 2000). New York: Henry Holt.

Greider, William. 1992. *Who Will Tell the People? The Betrayal of American Democracy.* New York: Simon & Schuster.

Gutman, Roy and David Rieff, eds. 1999. *Crimes of War: What the Public Should Know.* New York: W.W. Norton and Company.

Hamill, Sam, ed. 2003. *Poets Against the War.* New York: Thunder's Mouth Press.

Hayden, Tom. 1972. *The Love of Possession is a Disease With Them.* New York: Holt, Rinehart & Winston.

Ikenberry, G. John. 1989. *American Foreign Policy.* Washington, D.C.: Library of Congress.

Johnson, Chalmers. 2000. *Blowback: The Costs and Consequences of American Empire.* New York: Henry Holt and Company.

Johnson, Paul A. 1997. *A History of the American People.* New York: Harper & Prennial.

Johnson, Robert A. 1991. *Owning Your Own Shadow.* San Francisco: Harper Row.

Kennedy, Paul. 1987. *The Rise and Fall of the Great Powers.* New York: Random House.

Lapham, Lewis. 1998. *The Agony of Mammon.* New York: Verso.

———. 1998. *Waiting for the Barbarians.* New York: Verso.

Lazlo, Ervin. 1989. *The Inner Limits of Mankind.* London: Oneworld Pub.

Maguire, Peter. 2000. *Law and War: An American Story.* New York: Columbia University Press.

McGowan, David. 2000. *Derailing Democracy: The America the Media Don't Want You To See.* Monroe, ME: Common Courage Press.

Nevins, Allan and Henry Steele Commager. 1992. *Pocket History of the United States* (9th Ed.). New York: Pocket Books.

Power, Samantha. 2002. *"A Problem from Hell": America and the Age of Genocide.* New York: Basic Books.

Roy, Arundhati. 2003. *War Talk.* Cambridge, Massachusetts: South End Press.

Sheehan, Neil. 1988. *A Bright Shining Lie: John Paul Vann and America in Vietnam.* New York: Vintage Books.

Stannard, David E. 1992. *American Holocaust: Columbus and the Conquest of the New World.* Oxford: Oxford University Press.

Storr, Anthony, Ed. 1983. *The Essential Jung.* Princeton: Princeton University Press.

Striar, Margaret M. 1998. *Beyond Lament: Poets of the World Bearing Witness to the Holocaust.* Evanston, Illinois: Northwestern University Press.

Thompson, William Irwin. 1976. *Evil and World Order.* New York: Harper & Row.

Weitz, Eric D. 2003. *A Century of Genocide.* Princeton: Princeton University Press.

Wallerstein, Immanuel. 1998. *Utopistics.* New York: The New Press.

Yoneyama, Shoko. 1999. *The Japanese High School.* London and New York: Routledge.

Zinn, Howard. 1984. *The Twentieth Century: A People's History.* New York: Harper & Row Publishers.

> *And consciousness is the only sword which makes evil tremble.*
> — Ellen Hinsey

Part V – *Opposites: Testing and the Arts*

Testing: Great Is Our Sin

I) Books

Bok, Derek and William Bowen. 1998. *The Shape of the River: Long Term Consequensces of Considering Race in College and University Admissions.* Princeton: Princeton University Press.

Elmore, R.F. and R. Rothman, eds. 1999. *Testing, Teaching, and Learning: A Guide for States and School Districts.* Washington, DC: National Research Council.

Gardner, Howard. 2000. *The Disciplined Mind.* New York: Penguin Putnam.

Gould, Stephen Jay. 1996. *The Mismeasure of Man.* (Revised and Expanded). New York: W.W. Norton & Co.

Hernandez, Michele. 1997. *A is for Admission.* New York: Warner Books.

Heubert, J.P. and R. M. Hauser, eds. 1999. *High Stakes: Testing for Tracking, Promotion, and Graduation.* Washington, DC: National Research Council.

Jencks, Christopher. 1998. *The Black-White Test Score Gap.* Washington, DC: The Brookings Institute.

Kohn, Alfie. 2000. *The Case Against Standardized Testing: Raising the Scores, Ruining the Schools.* Portsmouth, New Hampshire: Heinemann.

Lemann, Nicholas. 1999. *The Big Test: The Secret History of the American Meritocracy.* New York: Farrar, Straus and Giroux.

McNeil, Linda M. 2000. *Contradictions of School Reform: Educational Costs of Standardized Testing.* London & New York: Routledge.

Meier, Deborah. 2000. *Will Standards Save Public Education?* Boston: Beacon.

Neill, M. et al. 1997. *Testing Our Children: A Report Card on State Assessment Systems.* Cambridge, Massachusetts: FairTest.

Ohanian, Susan. 1999. *One Size Fits Few: The Folly of Educational Standards.* Portsmouth, NH: Heinemann.

Sacks, Peter. 1999. *Standardized Minds: The High Price of America's Testing Culture and What We Can Do To Change It.* Cambridge, Mass: Perseus Books.

U.S. Department of Education, Office for Civil Rights. July 6, 2000. "The Use of Tests When Making High-Stakes Decisions for Students: A Resource Guide for Educators and Policymakers" (draft).

II) Articles

Adelman, Clifford. "Why Can't We Stop Talking About the SAT?" *The Chronicle of Higher Education*, Nov. 5, 1999, B4–B5.

Arenson, Karen W. "The Learning Gap." *Education Life Supplement, New York Times,* April 9, 2000.

Chase, Bob. "Cutting Class: Eliminating Electives Is Not A Smart Way to Raise Test Scores," *Education Week*, May 24, 2000, 35.

Clark M., W. Haney, and G. Madaus. "High Stakes Testing and High School Completion." Boston College, National Board on Educational Testing and Public Policy, January 2000.

Cuban, Larry. Feb. 18, 2001. "Two Decades of School Reforms Take Us Back to the 1950's." *Los Angeles Times*, M2–3.

Gardner, Howard. "The Testing Obsession." *Los Angeles Times*, Dec. 31, 2000, M1.

Greenberg, Daniel. "The Case Against Standardized Tests." *Paths of Learning*, Autumn 1999, 32–38.

Hirsch, E.D., Jr. "The Tests We Need: And Why We Don't Quite Have Them." *Education Week*, Feb. 2, 2000, 64, 40–41.

Hoff, David J. "Former DuPont Executive New Head of ETS." *Education Week*, July 12, 2000, 5.

Karen, David. "Scoring the SAT's." *The Nation*, Dec. 13, 1999, 40–44.

Kohn, Alfie. "Standardized Testing and Its Victims." *Education Week*, Sept. 27, 2000, 60, 46–47.

———. "Fighting the Tests." January 2001. *Phi Delta Kappan.*

Lemann, Nicholas and Ted Sizer, Linda Nathan and Angela Valenzuela. "Testing Mania: Good Intesntions Gone Awry." *Harvard Education Letter: Research On Line*, May/June, 2000.

McNeil, Linda. "The Educational Costs of Standardization." *Rethinking Schools*, Summer 2000, Vol. 14, No. 4, 8–9, 13.

McNeil, L.M. "Creating New Inequalities: Contradictions of Reform." *Phi Delta Kappan 81*, No. 10, June 2000, 729–734.

Meyers, Ellen and Frances O'Connell Rust. "The Test Doesn't Tell All." *Education Week*, May 31, 2000, 34–37.

Miner, Barbara. "Making the Grade." *The Progressive*, August 2000, 40–43.

Nathan, Linda. May/June 2000. *Harvard Education Letter.*

Natriello, G. and A.M. Pallas. "The Development and Impact of High-Stakes Testing." Paper presented at High Stakes K–12 Testing Conference sponsored by The Civil Right Project, Harvard University, December 1998.

Peterson, Bob. "Is There Value in Value-Added Testing?" *Rethinking Schools*, Summer 2000, Vol 14, No. 4, 1, 14–15.

Phillips-Fein, Kim. "The Meritocracy Trap." *Dissent*, Spring 2000, 113–116.

Prytowsky, Richard. "Testing Our Compassion and Insight." *Great Ideas in Education*, Psychology Press/Holistic Education Press, No. 17, Spring 2000, pp, 1–3, Corona, California.

Ryan, Alan. "The Twisted Path To The Top." *New York Review of Books*, (Review of Nicholas Lemann's *The Big Test*), Nov. 18, 1999, 20–25.

Roderick, M., A.S. Bryk, B.A. Jacob, J.Q. Easton, and E. Allensworth. "Ending Social Promotion: Results from the First Two Years." Consortium on Chicago School Research, December 1999.

Sadowski, Michael. "Are High-Stakes Tests Worth The Wager?" *Harvard Education Letter*, Sept./Oct. 2000, Vol. 16, No. 5.

Schrag, Peter. "High Stakes Are For Tomatoes." *The Atlantic Monthly*, August 2000, 19–21.

Schwartz, Tony. "The Test Under Stress." *The New York Times Magazine*, Jan. 10, 1999, 30–35.

Stoskopf, Alan. "SAT and ETS = $$$." *Rethinking Schools*, Spring 2000, 20–21.

Taylor, William L. "Standards, Tests, and Civil Rights." *Education Week*, Nov. 15, 2000, 56, 40–41.

Weissglass, Julian. "The SAT: Public-Spirited or Preserving Privilege?" *Education Week*, April 15, 1998, 60, 45.

> *You don't know what you don't know . . .*
> — Donald Rumsfeld
>
> *I'm the master of low expectations.*
> — George W. Bush

The Arts

Ackerman, Diane. 1990. *A Natural History of the Senses.* New York: Vintage.

Alpert, Herb. 2001. *Music for Your Eyes: Sculpture and Paintings.* Nashville, Tennessee: Tennessee State Museum.

Abrams, David. 1996. *The Spell of the Sensuous Perception and Language in a More-Than-Human World.* New York: Phatheon Books.

Bateson, G. 1972. *Steps to an Ecology of the Mind.* New York: Ballantine.

Berry, Thomas. 1999. *The Great Work: Our Way into the Future.* New York: Bell Tower.

Bloom, Benjamin, David R. Krathwohl and Bertram B. Masia. 1964. *Taxonomy of Educational Objectives: The Affective Domain.* New York: David McKay Company.

Bowers, C.A. 1993. *Critical Essays: On Education, Modernity, and the Recovery of the Ecological Imperative.* New York: Teachers College Press.

Bruner, Jerome S. 1966. *On Knowing: Essays for the Left Hand.* New York: Atheneum.

Cage, John. 1963. *A Year from Monday.* Middletown: Wesleyan University Press.

Cummins, Paul. 1992. *Dachau Song: The Twentieth Century Odyssey of Herbert Zipper.* New York: Peter Lang.

Dewey, John. 1934. *Art As Experience.* New York: Capricorn Books.

Dillard, Annie. 1982. *Teaching a Stone to Talk.* New York: Harper & Row.

Ghiselin, Brewster, ed. 1996. *The Creative Process.* New York: Mentor books.

Greene, Maxine. 2001. *Variations On A Blue Guitar.* New York: Teacher's College Press.

Lewis, Hilda Present. 1966. *Child Art: The Beginnings of Self-Affirmation.* Berkeley, California: Diablo Press.

Lindstrom, Miriam. 1960. *Children's Art.* Berkeley: University of California Press.

Madeja, Stanley S. and Sheila Onuska. 1977. *Through the Arts to the Aesthetic.* St. Louis: Cemrel.

May, Rollo. 1975. *The Courage to Create.* New York: Bantam Books.

Read, Herbert. 1948. *Education Through Art.* New York: Pantheon.

Robinson, Ken. 2001. *Out of Our Minds.* London: Capstone.

Rockefeller, David Jr. Chair. 1977. *Coming to our Senses: The Significance of the Arts in American Education.* New York: McGraw-Hill.

Upchurch, Carl. 1996. *Condemned in the Womb.* New York: Bantam Books.

Urgo, Joseph R. 2000. *In the Age of Distraction.* New York: Random House.

Whitehead, Alfred North. 1929. *The Aims of Education.* New York: The Macmillan Co.

> Art is the only true twin life has.
> — Charles Olsen

Question to poet Robert Creeley at a poetry reading:
Is that a real poem or did you make it up yourself?

Part VI – *New Forms of Engagement*

New Roads School

Boaz, David. Ed. 1991. *Liberating Schools: Education in the Inner City.* Washington, D.C. CATO Institute.

Bowers, C.A. 1995. *Educating for an Ecologically Sustainable Culture.* Albany: State University of New York Press.

Chomsky, Noam. 2000. *Chomsky on Miseducation.* Lanham, Maryland: Rowman and Littlefield Publishers.

Cummins, Paul F. and Anna Cummins. 1998. *For Mortal Stakes: Solutions for Schools and Society.* New York: Peter Lang Publishing Co. Las Vegas, Nevada: Bramble Books.

Cummins, Paul F. 2002. *Keeping Watch: Reflections on American Culture, Politics and Education.* Bloomington, Indiana: First Books Library.

Eisner, Elliot W. 1998. *The Kind of Schools We Need.* Portsmouth, New Hampshire: Heinemann.

Freire, Paolo. 1994. *Pedagogy of Hope.* New York: Continuum.

Greenberg, Daniel. 1987. *Free at Last: The Sudbury Valley School.* Farmington, Mass: The Sudbury Valley School Press.

Horenstein, MaryAnn. 1993. *Twelve Schools That Succeed.* Bloomington, Indiana: Phi Delta Kappa Educational Foundation.

Jervis, Kathe and Carol Montag, eds. 1991. *Progressive Education for the 1990s.* New York: Teachers College Press.

Nehring, James. 1998. *The School Within Us: The Creation of an Innovative Public School.* Albany, New York: State University of New York Press.

Orr, David W. 1994. *Earth in Mind: On Education, Environment, and the Human Prospect.* Washington, D.C.: Island Press.

Bibliography

Palmer, Parker J. 1998. *The Courage to Teach*. San Francisco: Jossey-Bass.

Rowlings, J.K. *The Harry Potter Series*. Five volumes. New York: Scholastic Press.

Schlechty, Phillip C. 1991. *Schools for the 21ˢᵗ Century*. San Francisco: Jossey-Bass Publishers.

Sleater, Christine E., ed. 1991. *Empowerment Through Multicultural Education*. Albany: State University of New York Press.

Tobin, Joseph J. David, Y.H. Wu, and Dana H. Davidson. 1989. *Preschool in three Cultures: Japan, China, and the United States*. New Haven: Yale University Press.

Toth, Jennifer. 1998. *Orphans of the Living: Stories of America's Children in Foster Care*. New York: Touchstone.

> *There is not a thing on earth without a star*
> *that beats upon it and tells it to grow.*
> — Stanley Moss, *Song of Imperfection*

The Educational Village

Bellah, Robert N. et al. 1992. *The Good Society.* New York: Vintage Books.

Bernstein, Nina. 2001. *The Lost Children of Wilder: The Epic Struggle to Change Foster Care.* New York: Pantheon Books.

Canada, Geoffrey. 1995. *Fist, Stick, Knife, Gun: A Personal History of Violence in America.* Boston: Beacon Press.

Cavallaro, Claire C. and Michelle Haney. 1999. *Preschool Inclusion.* Baltimore, MD: Paul H. Brooks Publishing Co.

Ceppi, Giulio & Michele Zini. 1998. *Children, Spaces, Relations: Meta Project for an Environment for Young Children.* Milan, Italy: Domus Academy Research Center.

Cohen, Shirley. 1998. *Targeting Autism.* Berkeley: University of California Press.

Coles, Robert. 1986. *The Moral Life of Children.* Boston: Houghton Mifflin.

Etzioni, Amitai. 1994. *The Spirit of Community.* New York: Touchstone.

Flinders, Carol Lee. 2002. *The Values of Belonging.* San Francisco: Harpercollins.

Haar, Sharon & Mack Robbins, eds. 2002. *Schools for Cities: Urban Statements.* New York: Princeton Architectural Press.

Koops, Willem and Michael Zuckerman, eds. 2003. *Beyond the Century of the Child.* Philadelphia: University of Pennsylvania Press.

Lane, Robert E. 2002. *The Loss of Happiness in Market Democracies.* New Haven: Yale University Press.

Maeroff, Gene I. 1998. *Altered Destinies: Making Life Better for School Children in Need.* New York: St. Martin's Press.

Polakow, Valerie. 2000. *The Public Assault on America's Children: Poverty,*

Violence and Juvenile Injustice. New York: Teacher's College Press.

Rose, Mike. 1989. *Lives on the Boundary.* New York: Penguin Books.

> *For last year's words belong to last year's language*
> *And next year's words await another voice.*
> — T.S. Eliot, *Little Gidding*

> *The new electronic interdependence recreates the world*
> *in the image of a global village.*
> — Marshall McLuhan

Conclusions

1) General Studies

Batchelor, Martin and Kerry Brown, eds. 1992. *Buddhism and Ecology.* Washington, DC.: World Wildlife Fund.

Diamond, Jared. 1997. *Guns, Germs, and Steel: The Fates of Human Societies.* New York: W.W. Norton & Company.

Halberstam, David. 1991. *The Next Century.* New York: William Morrow & Co.

Handy, Charles. 1998. *The Hungry Spirit Beyond Capitalism: A Quest for Purpose in the Modern World.* New York: Broadway Books.

Heilbroner, Robert. 1995. *Visions of the Future.* New York: Oxford University Press.

Krishnamurti, J. and David Bohm. 1986. *The Future of Humanity.* San Francisco: Harper & Row.

Lukacs, John. 1993. *The End of the Twentieth Century.* New York: Ticknor & Fields.

Marquez, Gabriel Garcia. Fall 1992. *Time Magazine.* Vol. 140, No. 27, 74.

Mohn, Reinhard. 2000. *Humanity Wins.* New York: Crown Business.

Snyder, Gary. 1995. *A Place in Space.* Washington, D.C.: Counterpoint.

Teilhard de Chardin. Quoted in Levitt, Peter. 1991. *Pablo Neruda Sky Stones.* Los Angeles: William Daily.

Thompson, William Irwin. 1974. *Passages About Earth: An Exploration of the New Planetary Culture.* New York: Harper and Row.

Wallerstein, Immanuel. 1998. *Utopistics: Or Historical Choices of the Twenty-First Century.* New York: The New Press.

Willkie, Wendell, L. 1943. *One World.* New York: Simon and Schuster.

II) 20th Century Histories

Bulliet, Richard W., ed. 1998. *The Columbia History of the Twentieth Century*. New York: Columbia University Press.

Conquest, Robert. 2000. *Reflections on a Ravaged Century*. New York: W.W. Norton & Co.

Gilbert, Martin. 1998. *A History of the Twentieth Century, Vols. I & II*. New York: William Morrow and Company, Inc.

Grenville, J.A.S. 1997. *A History of the World in the Twentieth Century, Vols. I & II*. Cambridge: The Balknap Press of Harvard University.

Hobsbawm, Eric. 1994. *The Age of Extremes: A History of the World, 1914–1991*. New York: Vintage Books.

Howard, Michael and William Roger Louis. 1998. *The Oxford History of the Twentieth Century*. New York: Alfred A. Knopf.

Johnson, Paul. 1991. *Modern Times: The World from the Twenties to the Nineties*. New York: Harper Perennial.

———. 1993. *Preparing for the Twenty-First Century*. New York: Random House.

Kennedy, Paul. 1987. *The Rise and Fall of the Great Powers*. New York: Random House.

Kolko, Gabriel. 1994. *Century of War: Politics, Conflicts and Society Since 1914*. New York: The New Press.

Lichtheim, George. 1972/1999. *Europe in the 20th Century*. London: Weidenfeld & Nicolson.

McNeill, William H. 1963/1991. *The Rise of the West*. Chicago: The University of Chicago Press.

III) New Stories

Berry, Thomas. 1988. *The Dream of the Earth.* Sierra Club Books.

Greider, William. 1997. *One World, Ready or Not.* New York: Touchstone.

Hayden, Tom. 1997. *The Lost Gospel of Earth.* San Francisco: Sierra Club Books.

Lovelock, J.E. 1979. *Gaia: A New Look at Life on Earth.* New York: Oxford University Press.

Mitchell, Stephen, Ed. 1993. *The Enlightened Heart.* New York: Harper Collins.

Neihardt, John G. 1972. *Black Elk Speaks.* New York: Washington Square Press.

Roszak, Theodore. 1973. *Where the Wasteland Ends.* New York: Anchor Books.

Sagan, Carl. 1973. *The Cosmic Connection: an Extraterrestrial Perspective.* New York: Anchor Books.

Slater, Philip. 1974. *Earthwalk.* New York: Anchor Press.

Swimme, Brian. 1984. *The Universe is a Green Dragon.* Santa Fe, New Mexico: Bear and Company.

Teilhard de Chardin, Pierre. 1959. *The Phenomenon of Man.* New York: Harper.

Thompson, William Irwin. 1974. *Passages About Earth.* New York: Harper and Row.

> *Sometime looking backward into this future, straining neck and eyes I'll meet your shadow with its enormous eyes. You who will want to know what this was all about . . .*
> — Adrienne Rich

Permissions

Cover Painting – "Coral Reef," by Herb Alpert. Permission granted by the artist.

"Doonesbury" c 2000 G.B. Trudeau. Reprinted with permission of Universal Press Synidcate. All rights reserved.

"The Downward Spiral" (Paul Cummins and Alva Libuser).

Photo. "Shifting Baselines." Permission from Randy Olson and the Ocean Conservancy.

"One nation divisible, with liberty and justice for some" (cartoon) by Paul Conrad. Published in the book *Paul Conrad: Drawing the Line.* Copyright, Tribune Media Services, Inc. All Rights Reserved. Reprinted with permission.

Cartoon. ©The New Yorker Collection 1989 Peter Steiner from cartoonbank.com. All Rights Reserved.

Cartoon. ©The New Yorker Collection 1992 Charles Barsotti from cartoonbank.com. All Rights Reserved.

Cartoon. ©The New Yorker Collection 2000 Tom Cheney from cartoonbank.com. All Rights Reserved.

Cartoon. ©The New Yorker Collection 1980 Ed Arno from cartoonbank.com. All rights Reserved.

Drawing. "Duck with Umbrella." Hugh Lofting. From the private collection of Paul Cummins.

Ecuador Painting. Anonymous Artist from Ecuador.

Diagram. "Failure of Leadership." Paul Cummins and Alva Libuser.

Painting. "Crossroads School." Permission of artist, Frank Romero.

Diagram. "Education." Paul Cummins and Alva Libuser.

Photo — "Las Iluminadas." By Christina Orci. Tzeltal women potters at a meeting of their cooperative "J'pas Lumetik" in 1994.

Photo – Juhae Son and Sergey Shepkin at a New Roads School piano master class, by David Weiss.

Painting: "Zipper Conducting," by Trudl Dubsky Zipper.

Painting: "Der Bucherwurm," by Carl Spitzweg.

Photo: "Joe Huber and Anna," by MaryAnn Cummins.

Photo: "Minako and Four Children," by Hiroko Yokota.

Drawing by Arthur Paunzen. From the private collection of the Herbert Zipper Room at the Paul Cummins Library of Crossroads School.

Photo (back cover): Paul, Anna and Emily by Mary Ann Cummins.

Biographical Notes

Paul F. Cummins, Ph.D.

Paul Cummins was born in Chicago, Illinois, moved to Fort Wayne, Indiana, and then to Los Angeles, California. He attended Stanford University (B.A., 1959), Harvard University (M.A.T., 1960), and the University of Southern California (Ph.D., 1967). He has taught English at Harvard School and the Oakwood School in California as well as at U.C.L.A. In 1970, he became the Headmaster of St. Augustine's Elementary School in Santa Monica and a Founder and Headmaster of the Crossroads School. In 1995, he was the lead founder of New Roads School and is currently the Executive Director of the New Visions Foundation.

His publications include a booklet on Richard Wilbur, several articles on education, and numerous poems which have appeared in journals including *The New Republic, Poetry LA, Whole Notes, Wild Bamboo Press, Bad Haircut Quarterly, Wordwrights, Slant*, and others. His biography on Herbert Zipper, *Dachau Song: The Twentieth-Century Odyssey of Herbert Zipper* (Peter Lang, 1992), has been translated into Chinese and German. *For Mortal Stakes: Solutions for Schools and Society*, was published in 1998 by Peter Lang Publishing and Bramble Books and was also published in Japan. *Keeping Watch: Reflections On American Culture, Education and Politics* was published by Firstbooks Library in 2002. Argonne Press issued a collection of poetry, *A Postcard from Bali*, also in 2002. An essay, "The Vital Left," appeared in *Fake City Syndrome*, published by Red Hen Press in 2002.

Cummins serves on the board of trustees of the American Poetry Review, Camino Nuevo Charter Academy, ExEd, the Sam Francis Foundation, the Gabriella Axelrad Foundation, New Roads School, and the New Visions Foundation. He and his wife, Mary Ann, live in Santa Monica, California. They have four daughters.

Anna K. Cummins

Anna K. Cummins graduated from Crossroads School in Santa Monica in 1991, and Stanford University in 1996 with a B.A. in History. At Stanford, she studied with Dr. Estelle Friedman (Women's Studies), Dr. Jody Maxmin (Art History) and Dr. Jack Rakove (American History). Also at Stanford, she was captain of the fencing team in 1994 and performed in chamber music concerts on the violin. She taught at New Roads School in Santa Monica in 1996 and received her M.A. in International Environmental Policy at the Monterey Institute for International Studies in California in 2002. She co-authored *For Mortal Stakes: Solutions For Schools and Society*, co-published in 1998 by Peter Lang and Bramble Books. Anna is currently working for Save Our Shores in Santa Cruz, California.

Emily Cummins

Emily Cummins graduated from Northwestern University in 1998 with a B.A. in History. At Northwestern she played varsity softball, played cello in a university orchestra, and made Dean's List majoring in History. She worked at New Roads School from 1998-1999 and then traveled throughout South America with her sister, Anna. She received her M.S.W. from UCLA in June of 2002, and is currently a social worker in the Lennox School District in Los Angeles.

The eyes of the future are looking back at us and praying for us to see beyond our own time . . .
—Terry Tempest Williams